Official
Hakko Denshin Ryu
Ju Jutsu

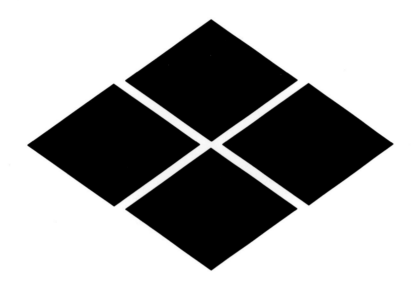

Study Guide
And
Training Manual
Shodan

Michael J. LaMonica
Director and Chief Instructor
Hakko Denshin Ryu Ju Jutsu USA
USA Honbu (Headquarters), Akron, Ohio

First Edition

Published by:
 HDJF Publishing
1177 S. Hametown Road
Copley, Ohio

This Hakko Denshin Ryu Ju Jutsu manual was written by Michael J. LaMonica, Kaiden Shihan San Dai Kichu.

ISBN: 0-9722965-0-6

Printed in the United States by BookMasters, Inc.

To order this book...

Send Check and Order to:

HDJF Publishing
1177 S. Hametown Road
Akron, Ohio 44321
USA

On your order please include:
Number of books
Name
Shipping address
Telephone number and E–mail address

Check-out our web-sight at: http://www.hakkojujutsu.com

Disclaimer: All of these techniques should be performed under the supervision of a sanctioned HDJF Black Belt. The author and publisher of this book are not responsible in any manner or for any reason for any possible injury that may occur through reading and following the waza and instructions throughout this manual.

Michael J. LaMonica is one of those exceptional people. A man with experience, enthusiasm, and leadership qualities that 28 years of law enforcement has sharpened to the man he is today.

Mike was born one of three (3) children in Akron, Ohio. His parents were born in Akron, Ohio and his father worked all his life in Akron, Ohio.

In 1959, young Michael joined the City of Akron's Police Department where he stayed for 21 years, working as a patrolman, in the Detective Bureau, Department of Community Relations, in command of Intelligence Unit, S.W.A.T. Unit, and as assistant Director of the Training Bureau. During these 21 years, Mike earned himself a reputation as a dedicated public servant, and an officer anyone would be honored to have as a partner. Mike also received many awards for Police Heroism and Public Service. Among his best assignments, besides teaching young law enforcement students, both at the Police Academy and at the University of Akron, was guarding VIPs that flowed through the City of Akron and North Eastern Ohio.

Mike worked with the Secret Service, the FBI, and County Agencies during political visits and also guarded people such as Danny Thomas, who came to Ohio for fund raisers and personal appearances. These duties placed Mike in contact with Presidents Reagan, Carter, Nixon and Kennedy, and Governors Celeste and Rhodes of Ohio, and many others that came to Ohio; plus many other show business figures.

Michael LaMonica, a strapping man of 6'4", is not only a "crackshot", but in the opinion of his fellow officers, can handle the toughest of the tough.

In May 1980, LaMonica left his post with the Akron Police Department to take on yet another challenge, Chief of the Fairlawn Police Department. Although this community is small in population, it is the fastest growing commercial area in Summit County, Ohio.

Along with his dedicated Police work, Mike has raised his family of five (5) children, all girls, His wife, Chris, is a 7th Degree Black Belt in Ju Jutsu.

LaMonica has also received many honors over the years. Some of which were:

- Knight Cavalier – National Association of Chiefs of Police

- Liberty & Justice Award - National Association of Chiefs of Police

- Special Citation Award - National Association of Chiefs of Police

- Jaycee Man of The Year - 1972

- 113th Session—FBI National Academy Section Representative

- Master Firearms Award – 1978 FBI Academy

About the Author and Soke of Hakko Denshin Ryu Ju Jutsu North and South America

- Vice President Ohio Association of Chief of Police

- Hakko Ryu Ju Jutsu – Rank of Menkyo Kaiden, Shihan, San Dai Kichu – The highest ranking non-oriental in the world

- World Ju Jutsu Federation – Ninth Degree Black Belt

- Second Degree Black Belt – Judo

- Black Belt – Chinese Kempo

As the first non-Japanese to ever receive the highest rank for technical excellence, San Dai Kichu (three great pillars), he is often relied upon for council by the founder of Hakko Ryu, Ryuho Okuyama. So trusted is he that in August of 1981, he received a certificate naming him as a personal advisor to Mr. Okuyama, and Director for North America for Hakko Ryu Ju Jutsu. Mr. Okuyama has recently passed away.

Mike began his martial arts training while serving in the Marine Corps in the late 1950's. Then in the 1960's, he had an opportunity to meet the man who introduced Hakko Ryu to the United States, James A. Benko. As a Police Officer, he quickly saw the value of Hakko Ryu techniques for law enforcement.

Mike began training with Mr. Benko shortly after they met, and continued until 1975 when he was invited by the Okuyama family to live with them as an uchideshi (inside deciple). Upon completion of his study, he was awarded the certificate and makimono (hand scroll) of Shihan (master instructor license). In 1979, at the invitation of Mr. Okuyama, Mike returned to Japan to

complete the most advanced training given in Hakko Ryu, and was awarded the Menkyo Kaiden License and San Dai Kichu (three great pillars) makimono.

Mike, together with his wife Chris (who was the first non-Japanese woman to receive Shihan in Hakko Ryu) teach various law enforcement agencies in Ohio, and Mike has served as an instructor at the FBI Academy. To compliment his Hakko Ryu and police experience, Mike trained in Tokyo with the Dai Yon Kidootai (#4 Riot Police) under Tsunemori Kaminoda. Additionally, he studied jo (short staff) techniques under Kaminoda and Shimizu and Senseis Masakiryu Manrikigusari (10000-power chain) under Yumio Nawa Sensei. In the United States, Mike is a graduate of the FBI Academy. He also completed the FBI course in Anti-Sniper and Survival Tactics, and training from U.S. Secret Service Dignitary Protection School Instructors.

At present, Mike is the Founder, Director, and Chief Instructor of the North and South America Hakko Denshin Ryu Ju Jutsu.

A Special Thanks to Brian Workman and James A. Benko

Contents

- Hakko Dori

- Atemi

- Aiki Nage

- Te Kagami

- Hiza Gatame

- Ude Osae Dori

- Mune Osae Dori

- Uchi Komi Dori

- Yoko Kata Te Osae Dori

- Yoko Moro Te Osae Dori / Kiza Dori

- Hakko Zeme

Contents

- Tachi Ate

- Hiki Nage

- Te Kagami

- Ude Osae Dori

- Mune Osae Dori

- Ryo Ude Osae Dori

- Ryo Mune Osae Dori

- Uchi Komi Dori

- Ushiro Zeme Otoshi

- Kubi Shime Dori

Forward

This text was written by Kaiden Shihan Sandai Kichu Michael J. LaMonica, Director and Soke of the Hakko Denshin Ryu Ju Jutsu Federation. Hakko Ryu Founder Ryuho Okuyama's Direct Shihan and Hakko Ryu Mimawari-Yaku, USA. It has been updated to include changes made by Honbu, additional historical information, expanded sections on Koho Shiatsu and Japanese terminology, and is in a somewhat different format. With those exceptions, it is exactly as Mr. Benko wrote in 1969. We have also expanded this manual to include the transformation of Hakko Ryu Ju Jutsu into Hakko Denshin Ryu.

Special thanks to the following and without whom this project could not have been completed:

Editing and layout:

Cristine Kobak

Chris Kobak

Preface

The aim of this training manual on Hakko Denshin Ryu Ju Jutsu is to provoke an interest in the reader to learn more about this particular system of self-defense. This manual may be used as a text for beginning students in the art. Every fact contained herein is important to the student, since many Hakko Denshin Ryu instructors will make use of this manual to create promotional examination questions.

In the United States, Hakko Denshin Ryu Ju Jutsu is taught by members of the Hakko Denshin Ryu Ju Jutsu Federation (United States branch). If you are not a student of Hakko Denshin Ryu and would like to be, write to the HDJF Headquarters for the address of the Hakko Denshin Ryu Ju Jutsu school nearest you. If you are an instructor of a martial art which is similar to Hakko Denshin Ryu or Ko Ko Do Ju Jutsu and interested in learning and eventually teaching Hakko Denshin Ryu Ju Jutsu, special training arrangements and considerations can be made for you. Please write to HDJF Headquarters:

MICHAEL J. LAMONICA

1177 South Hametown Road

Akron, Ohio, USA

44321

History of Hakko Denshin Ryu Ju Jutsu

HISTORY OF HAKKO-RYU JU-JUTSU

ALTHOUGH HAKKO-RYU JU-JUTSU WAS FOUNDED in 1941, it inherits a centuries-old legacy of classical bujutsu (warrior arts) used by the samurai of feudal Japan. Indeed, Hakko-ryu founder Ryuho Okuyama (1901-1987) and his son Nidai Soke Ryuho (Toshio) Okuyama come from a long line of prominent bushi (warriors), the Genji clan. As a student of Hakko-ryu, you can trace the origins of your art as far back as the 8th Century A.D.

Although there are sketchy references to martial art techniques dating as far back as 23 B.C., the first generally acknowledged Japanese grappling system was developed by Prince Teijun Fujiwara, sixth son of Japan's 56th Emperor Seiwa who was given the name Minamoto. His descendants are known as the Seiwa Genji and his aikijutsu techniques were kept as a secret family art. With them, the Minamoto clan rose to become the most powerful warriors in all of Japan in only four generations.

MASTER OF MANY ARTS

Among the most famous of the Seiwa Genji was General Yoshimitsu Shinra Saburo Minamoto. He was a master of many arts: warrior, poet, physician and historian. He greatly advanced the arts of atemi (striking vital points) and kansetsu (joint locks) by

dissecting and analyzing the bodies of criminals and war dead. He lived in the Daito mansion, which many believe to be how the Minamoto style of Aiki-jutsu came to be called Daito-ryu. General Yoshimitsu passed on the techniques to his son Yoshimitsu Yoshikiyu, who resided in Takeda in the province of Kai.

Near the end of the 16th century, the Takeda Han fought the formation of the Tokugawa Shogunate, which was destined to rule Japan until the Meiji Restoration in 1868. When the position of the Kai Takeda became untenable, the family moved north to take up services in the Aizu Han where they became known as the Aizu Takeda. There they held the position of shinamban (clan fencing masters) and taught their art to the clan's most senior members. The last of the Aizu shinamban, Takeda Takumi no Kami Minamoto Soemon (1758-1853), had two important students. One was Takeda Soyoshi, his grandson. The other, Saigo Tanamo (1829-1905) was minister of the Aizu Han and head of Shirakawa Castle. In 1868, when the Meiji Restoration returned power to the emperor, Soyoshi was killed as a leader of the resistance to this change. Saigo became a Shinto

History of Hakko Denshin Ryu Ju Jutsu

priest at the Nikko Toshugu shrine, changing his name to Hoshino Genshin. His senior student was Takeda Sokichi, Soyoshi's eldest son. When Sokichi died in 1875, Saigo called his younger brother to the shrine to continue the Minamoto tradition.

CONTINUING THE TRADITION

Enter Takeda Sokaku Minamoto Masayoshi (1858-1943), the last of the great swordsmen. Here was a man who lived, breathed, ate, slept and dreamt the martial arts. His fanatical devotion is perhaps explained as a compensation for the fact that, at less than five feet tall, he was much smaller than his elder brother. Born and raised as a samurai, Sokaku began his study of Daito-ryu aiki ju jutsu and Ono-ha itto-ryu kenjutsu (swordsmanship) at the age of five. His tremendous natural abilities and small size soon earned him the name of kotengu (little demon).

By the age of 20, he had earned licenses from four of the most highly respected sword and spear schools in Japan. For the next 20 years, he traveled throughout Japan issuing challenges, and was rarely defeated. He is said to be one of the few people ever to master all 18 of the traditional martial arts. Sokaku was not yet ready for temple life, however, and left after only six months.

Saigo then selected Shida Shiro (1868-1920). While in

History of Hakko Denshin Ryu Ju Jutsu

Tokyo in 1881, Shiro met Jigoro Kano, who was in the process of creating a new organization called Kodokan Judo. Shiro joined him and quickly became the most senior member. He was appointed director of the Kodokan in 1888, but soon was overcome with the conflict of loyalties between Judo and Daito-ryu. In 1891, he deserted both systems and Saigo Tanamo once again called on Takeda Sokaku, hoping he would now be ready. Finally, in 1898, Tanamo managed to convince Sokaku to assume the leadership of the Daito-ryu. Sokaku's years of intensive training had established a life-pattern, however, that could not be broken. He traveled Japan teaching, never stopping long enough to establish his own dojo. His students were among northern Japan's elite: generals, Admirals, judges and mayors. By 1915, he was the most famous instructor north of Tokyo. Daito-ryu Aiki ju jutsu survives to this day, under the leadership of Sokaku's son, Takeda Tokimune. Also among Sokaku's chief instructors was Toshimi Hosaku Matsuda, who taught one of his more gifted students extensively in the techniques of the ryu. This student would later study directly under the guidelines of Sokaku Takeda himself.

This student's name was Okuyama Yoshiharu (Yoshiji) also known as Ryuho Okuyama, founder of Hakko-ryu Ju-jutsu.

OUT OF THE MIST **

Okuyama Yoshiharu (Yoshiji) was born on February 21,1901, in Yachi-cho, Nishi Mura-

History of Hakko Denshin Ryu Ju Jutsu

yama, Yamagata Prefecture, to a former samurai family of the upper Mogami River area. Not a great deal is known about his earlier years except that he was active in various bujutsu-ryu (martial arts systems) and studied traditional Oriental Medicine.

In 1924, he entered one of the most prestigious government training schools of the day called the Tokyo Seiji Gakko (Tokyo School of Government), where he soon excelled as an orator. By the time he graduated in 1927, he was distinguished as the Prime Minister to the First Oratorical Imperial Youth's Congress.

Upon his graduation he struck out to the frontier of Japan, Hokkaido, where he hoped to quickly make his mark. It was here at Asahikawa, through his contacts in government work, that he first became introduced to Shihan Toshimi (Hosaku) Matsuda, who at that time was teaching Daito-ryu Aiki jujutsu at the Shobukan Dojo. Matsuda, a tough Japanese, born in Hokkaido and former apprentice to the founder of Daito-ryu, Shihan Somi (Sokaku) Takeda, soon found that Mr. Okuyama was an excellent student, and taught him extensively the techniques of the ryu.

MANY TEACHERS

During his travels, Okuyama had the opportunity to stay with various teachers, and picked up a

considerable amount of knowledge and perspective in the process. One of his major areas of interest was traditional Oriental medical therapy, and on several occasions he was able to apprentice himself to some highly skilled teachers. The first was Ryozan Hirayama, whom Mr. Okuyama first met in 1930. Hr. Hirayama was a teacher and practitioner of the Japanese In/Yo (Chinese Yin/Yang) therapy as applied to keiraku therapy (circulation medicine using the meridians of the body), who

taught Mr. Okuyama its principles and application to the diagnosis of disease, both pulse and ninso (face reading), shiatsu (finger pressure medicine), amma (massage) and diet. Mr. Okuyama also studied one of the more esoteric schools of therapy of the time, western medicine, under Haizan Minami, whom he first met in 1934, and with whom he became close friends from that time forward.

Among the martial arts other than Daito-ryu studied during his pilgrimages, the major ones included Hasegawako-ryu iaijutsu (sword drawing), which he learned from Shihan Kiichi Yama-

History of Hakko Denshin Ryu Ju Jutsu

guchi in the city of Sapporo; Shurikenjutsu (various throwing weapons) and jojutsu (sticks) from teachers in the mountains of Niigata; kusari-gama (sickle-chain) in Ise; Nito-ryu kenjutsu (sword) and kyujutsu (archery) in his home province of Yamagata.

In 1936, Mr. Okuyama was awarded the instructor's license in Daito-ryu and thereafter apprenticed himself to Shihan Somi Takeda, where he studied the Okuden (secret techniques), and assisted Takeda with the day -to -day running of his aiki association. At the time, Takeda was quite old, well over 80 (Mr. Okuyama described him as "completely toothless, but robust for a man his age"), and needed help with a great many things. For a while, Mr. Okuyama was personally responsible for all of Takeda's assets, which could have been rather formidable considering he charged the equivalent of $150 and $259 per technique, depending on the level of training one desired. At the time, there were three levels of training -- shoden (basic), chuden (middle), and okuden (secret) -- and four sets of basic techniques numbering 582. The higher the level, the more a student needed to pay.

History of Hakko Denshin Ryu Ju Jutsu

Given this, one may readily see why the founder of Aikido, Morihei Uyeshiba, who trained formally with Takeda for a total of 100 days before receiving the instructor's license, gave up his entire inheritance. Keep in mind, however, that Takeda's family, former Otome-ryu kenjutsu instructors of the Aizu clan, were put completely out of work after the dismantling of Japan's feudal system during the Meiji Restoration of 1868. He, like so many of his contemporaries, sold his martial arts skills to the public in order to make a living, a pattern that continues in certain ryu today. This was less objectionable to some former samurai than taking a pedestrian job.

MR. OKUYAMA'S FIRST DOJO

Upon finishing his studies with Takeda in 1938, Mr. Okuyama published the first of what was to be one of many martial arts texts entitled "Daito-ryu Goshinjutsu" (The Daito System of Self-protection). Shortly thereafter, backed by the assistance of Army General Iwane Matsui and Naval Attache Kumpei Matsumoto, Mr. Okuyama established the Dai-Nippon Shidokai (Greater Japan Way of the Samurai Association) and became a public instructor in what he called Daito-ryu Hiden Shido (Secret Daito-ryu Way of the Samurai). His first dojo was in Asahikawa and was called the Nippon Shidokai Ryubukan.

In 1939, he moved to the Kanda district in Tokyo and founded the Dai Nihon Shidokai, which be-

History of Hakko Denshin Ryu Ju Jutsu

gan his split from the main Daito-ryu school. By this time, Takeda was too old to take care of himself and the leadership of Daito-ryu was somewhat in question. The heir apparent, Tokimune Takeda, was still quite young, but seemed destined to take over the ryu. Mr. Okuyama, seeing little chance for administrative advancement in Daito-ryu, grew restless. After so many years of study and travel, he had become a highly skilled exponent of both martial arts and medicine, and wanted to use those skills not only to bring financial benefits and fame for himself, but also to be of distinguished service to his country. It was this environment that he began to formulate his own distinct system.

"THE SPINE OF THE DRAGON"

Finally, on June 1,1941, at the Shiba Tenso Jinja (Shinto shrine in the Shiba district of Tokyo), he held the Hakko-ryu Kaiso Hokoku-sai [Ceremony Proclaiming to the Kami (Shinto deities) the Birth of Hakko-ryu]. From that day forward, Mr. Okuyama took the pen name of Ryuho, meaning "the spine of the dragon" and called his system Hakko-ryu Ju Jutsu.

History of Hakko Denshin Ryu Ju Jutsu

During the war, he taught Hakko-ryu in its original form to many of the leaders in government and the military and in 1943 renamed his dojo the Hakko-ryu Kobujuku (Private School of the Ancient Martial Art Hakko-ryu). He was featured in magazines, gave seminars and appeared on radio talk shows.

By the middle of the decade, however, the war situation began to look increasingly bleak, and with the continuous Allied bombings, Tokyo was becoming almost uninhabitable. Finally, in 1945, Mr. Okuyama abandoned the Kanda dojo and escaped to his home prefecture of Yamagata. The trip was very difficult. Mr. Okuyama wrote of having to subsist on a single piece of tofu each day, and sleeping in the snow with only an amado (storm door made of light wood) for shelter. One can hardly imagine the difficulties faced by the average Japanese citizen during that period. Once arrived, he and a small group of followers joined the Mt. Haguro sect of Shugendo where they prayed for peace and the deliverance of the nation.

In 1947, Mr. Okuyama quietly relocated to Saitama Prefecture where he established the Hakko Juku Honbu Dojo (Private Headquarters Dojo of Hakko-ryu) and slowly rebuilt his former life as a martial arts teacher and healer. By this time, his political aspirations had been completely destroyed, and he decided to leave that era of his life behind him. In this post-war environment, however, making a living as a martial artist was not an easy task, either; but gradually, over many

years, he succeeded in doing so.

A PHILOSOPHY OF "COMMON SENSE"

Both the techniques and philosophy evolved until ultimately Hakko-ryu took its current form as a modern martial art (shin-bujutsu) which, in its essence, strives to create more justice in society through the introduction of humanitarian principles of self-protection. The groundwork for this was laid before the war and combined both medical and martial techniques. Through use of the meridian system of the body, a Hakko-ryu exponent can deliver varying amounts of pain to control the attacker, usually without causing serious injury. This is a distinguishing characteristic of Hakko-ryu, and has won strong backing in the Japanese law enforcement profession.

Since that time and until his death in 1987, Mr. Okuyama developed a solid following for his system. His method of teaching students individually, or in smal groups, added to the uniqueness of Hakko-ryu and assisted in building its reputation. His son, Toshio Okuyama, is now Headmaster of the ryu and continues, for the most part, in his father's original pattern. Hakko-ryu is one of the very few authentic jujutsu ryu which has been successful in establishing roots outside of the islands of Japan.

It was Mr. Okuyama's goal to see the philosophy of Hakko-ryu accepted as the "common

History of Hakko Denshin Ryu Ju Jutsu

sense of mankind," and although the road is very long, this one man, during a very turbulent period, was able to travel a great distance.

A PEACETIME MARTIAL ART SCHOOL

Since Ryuho Okuyama founded Hakko-ryu in 1941, the international headquarters of Hakko-ryu has moved to Omiya City, (now called Saitama City) in Japan's Saitama Prefecture. By the end of World War II, Hakko-ryu had completely evolved into a peacetime martial art school in Omiya City and international branch schools. Millions have heard the word of Hakko-ryu through lectures and demonstrations throughout the world.

Hakko (Eighth Light) was the name which Mr. Okuyama thoughtfully assigned to his school of jujutsu. Hakko, in the manner used by Mr. Okuyama, reflects great national pride, while it explains a main concept of his style of self defense. He philosophically conceived that there are nine color bands in the sun's color spectrum. The eighth of these nine bands, which he refers to as a shade of red, holds the secret of the power of Hakko-ryu Ju Jutsu. This eighth light of which Mr. Okuyama speaks is seemingly very weak in composition; but is fact, it is surprisingly powerful. Red, as he used it, symbolizes the land of the rising sun -- Japan. He goes on to explain that the ninth band, the color purple, creates and develops the eighth light. Purple is the color of royalty and honor in Japan.

A NEW BEGINNING

History of Hakko Denshin Ryu Ju Jutsu

On August 5, 1997 Menkyu Shihan Kaiden San Dai Kichu's Michael J. LaMonica, Yasuhiro Irie, and Antonio Garcia formed Hakko Denshin Ryu Ju Jutsu and KoKoDo Renmei. At present Michael J. LaMonica has been named the Soke of Hakko Denshin Ryu. Yasuhiro Irie is Soke of KoKoDo Ju Jutsu International and Antonio Garcia is Doshu of Europe.

Philosophy and Intent

GENTLENESS

Ju is construed to mean gentleness, lovingness, softness, yielding and like words. In Hakko-ryu (Eighth Light School), students learn to yield to the strength of assailants. Moreover, all of the Jutsu (arts of) Hakko-ryu are systematically devised to enable students to be gentle and loving with assailants. We, of Hakko-ryu, feel that this fact distinguishes Hakko-ryu Jutsu from other popular martial art systems.

NO STRENGTH

Even before their first lesson, students of Hakko-ryu are instructed to abandon their physical strength. This is accomplished by a process of mere relaxation. If a student abandons their strength, they naturally yield to the strength of an assailant. However, this concept of no strength extends even further. Students are taught to relax even when applying Hakko-ryu techniques. If, when doing a technique, a student resorts to strength, they are doing the technique incorrectly. It is not necessary to be strong to use Hakko-ryu techniques effectively. Therefore, Hakko-ryu techniques can be used immediately by anyone, young or old, male or female.

Since the application of Hakko-ryu techniques does not require strength, they are not difficult to master. Mr. Okuyama, in creating Hakko-ryu, wanted techniques that could be applied with natural movements. A natural movement is instinctive and requires no special training to develop.

Philosophy and Intent

Most Hakko-ryu techniques are as easy as scratching an itchy ear, kneeling on one knee, or extending a finger. In most budo (martial way) schools, it takes a great deal of time to master tricky movements which require strength and great skill.

In a Hakko-ryu dojo (training place), students practice the easy techniques again and again. Each time they practice a technique, they try to abandon more of their strength and become completely relaxed. This is the conditioning method of instinctive relaxation. When a person is relaxed, they can think more clearly. A person under tension sometimes uses his mind as a muscle and loses self-control. Instinctive relaxation extends beyond the realm of self-defense into everyday activities. Everyone should learn and practice this theory to aid him/her in acting prudently in tense situations. To develop the art of instinctive relaxation, a person must be consciously trained until they are unconsciously relaxed.

A person on the receiving end of a skin pinch would discover that if he relaxes when the pinch is administered, there would be very little pain. Additionally, a person completely relaxed is like dead weight and cannot easily be moved about. This idea can be compared to an intoxicated person who falls or is bumped hard enough that a sober person would feel a great deal of pain. The

Philosophy and Intent

intoxicated person is definitely relaxed and feels no pain. When a ruffian attacks, he is bound to use strength. Consequently, he is more vulnerable than someone who is relaxed. If the innocent party were to defend with strength, they would be opposed with strength from the ruffian. In such cases, the strongest would win.

Ruffians are experienced in using strength to fight strength. But what if they were opposed with no strength? Would they know what to do? You can try the gentle theory of no strength with a friend. Attempt to take your friend through a doorway by using strength to pull and push him. You will discover that this is a very difficult task, because he will oppose you with strength. Later, merely walk up to his side and very slowly touch his upper arm gently with your hand. Then, walk toward the doorway and chat with him the whole time. You will discover that the second method is much easier.

NO INJURY

If, when attacked, an individual desires to protect himself by not injuring the assailant, it is really a mark of refinement. Since Hakko-ryu techniques have not yet reached most of the world's population, knowledge of gentle self-defense techniques is severely limited. On the other hand, knowledge of self-defense techniques which injure or kill is overabundant. A person could name hundreds of ways to injure of kill. He could direct his hands, elbows, feet, knees, blunt instruments, or

mechanical instruments to various vital points of their assailant's body. It would be a perplexing task to name just a couple of ways to rid himself of an assailant without injuring him. Hakko-ryu techniques are specifically designed to enable refined humanitarians to defend without injury.

This fact qualifies Mr. Okuyama to adopt a moral code to be adhered to by all his students. The gentle techniques of Hakko-ryu are designed to only discourage or capture assailants or offenders. "An eye for an eye" does not pertain to Hakko-ryu Ju Jutsu, the most gentle of all popular self-defensive arts.

NO COMPETITION

Since Hakko-ryu techniques are completely defensive and humanitarian in nature, students are never taught to attack. Hakko-ryu techniques are not used in competitive sport. In any competitive sport, there must be an equal amount of offense and defense. When budo schools become sport-minded , they are no longer self-defense schools. They are offense/defense schools.

The dangers of sport budo are numerous. If the offensive techniques taught in sport budo fell into the hands of a person who would use them on innocent people, he would be well-versed in the art

of attack. Or if an evil person were to watch a competitive budo event, he could easily remember techniques of most budo schools and use them on whomever he wished. Since the techniques of most budo schools are intended to injure or destroy assailants, they are dangerous in the wrong

hands. For that matter, they are even dangerous in the right hands, since they are like deadly weapons. Improper or proper use of them usually injures assailants, opponents, or even innocent parties.

In many cases, budo competition results in bloodshed, broken bones, internal injuries and unconsciousness. From the humanitarian point of view, commercialism has turned these once honorable self-defense arts into violent fights. Onlookers cannot be blamed for not trying to learn self-defense in this rough and tumble fashion. Why should people be bloodied up and bounced around to learn how to prevent themselves from being bloodied up and bounced around? It just does not make sense. Refined people who do not like rough-and-tumble methods of self-defense should come to an Eighth Light School. Since there is no injury delivered to assailants from Hakko-ryu students, a student playing the role of the assailant in practice will never be injured. Honorable budo schools that are now competition-minded should do away with these fights and devise new ways to teach their techniques. The

longer that budo competition continues, the more intense the fighting will become and the more injuries will be sustained.

DANGERS OF BRUTAL TECHNIQUES

What goes through the minds of impressionable youngsters who view violent techniques? They see the hero, or "good guy", brutally knock or throw his opponent, or the "bad guy", to the ground. The loser lays unconscious as spectators cheer. Would a youngster be the "good guy" by violently striking or throwing a schoolmate who gets in his way? Naturally, we would like for our sons and daughters to be able to defend themselves. But, must they use violent techniques when gentle techniques are available at an Eighth Light School? When society condones violence as fit for the eyes and ears of youngsters, it is society who is responsible for the influence that violence gives.

The arresting, searching and self-defense techniques used by police are of prime importance to every citizen. Should they act as the judge and jury, by administering a violent penalty when arresting offenders, because they lack the knowledge of gentle techniques? Or should they use techniques that are completely gentle (preserving civil rights), which can be mastered quickly (saving taxpayers money for extensive training)?

Hakko-ryu is the perfect art for police.

Philosophy and Intent

The opposition of violence with violence does not stop violence. It only creates and breeds more violence. Forms of violence have been part of society since ancient times. Nevertheless, that does not mean that there is no need for a change. If the world gives up and declares gentleness a dead virtue, society will suffer.

EXCEPTIONAL CIRUMSTANCES

Some experts of traditional martial arts have argued that Hakko-ryu Ju Jutsu is an advanced form of self-defense that can only be appreciated by those who have practiced martial arts for many years. They say that a new student should first learn a type of martial art

that stresses serious injury. This approach will supposedly instill confidence in the new student. They go on to say that there are circumstances in which complete gentleness cannot be used. Such instances would be attacks by three or more assailants and combat situations of "kill or be killed". Each of these observations is a good one. However, Hakko-ryu Ju Jutsu is not as important in providing the necessary elements of a martial art as some people might believe. Remember, the meaning of the name "Hakko-ryu". The name infers deceptive power.

NEW STUDENTS

Even a person untrained in martial knows many ways to injure. For the most part, these ways are vicious strikes to vital points in the body. Therefore, to build a new student's confidence in his ability to inflict injury, a Hakko-ryu instructor should ask him to demonstrate techniques that he already knows that will cause injury. Of course, everyone knows how to deliver injury. Hence, there is no need to teach students how to inflict more injuries. However, there is a problem in putting an assailant in such a position, in which he cannot injure you while you are injuring him.

Hakko-ryu techniques are designed to render assailants helpless with stunning and controlling techniques. If the user of Hakko-ryu techniques felt that it was necessary to use vicious blows on an assailant while the assailant was in a helpless state, it would be his prerogative. Regretfully, there are exceptional circumstances in which assailants must be injured.

If a person trains intensely to do as much damage as possible in the shortest amount of time, it is difficult for him to practice gentleness. He is conditioned to instinctively respond to attacks with devastating techniques. This is not right! A martial art student should be trained, from the beginning, to respond to attacks with gentleness. If gentleness does not work for some reason, then a

little more force should be used. In exceptional situations, mild injury may have to be delivered. However, the situations which permit mild injury are definitely "exceptional". A push, clothing seizure, or blow with a hand or weapon, are not exceptional circumstances if they are delivered by only one person at a time. The only two times that complete gentleness may not do the job are group attacks and combat situations.

GROUP ATTACKS

Hakko-ryu techniques will stun, discourage and capture assailants. A student could confidently use gentle techniques on one or two assailants. However, he will have some problems in being completely gentle when attacked by three or more assailants. Suppose he stuns each assailant with atemi waza, a throwing technique, or wrist bend. When the last of the assailants is being stunned, the first assailant may be attacking again. After being stunned once or twice, a few of the assailants may be discouraged from attacking again. But this might not always be the case.

Mr. Okuyama's approach to this problem is to discourage the leader of the group first, for it is reasonable to assume that the members of a group of ruffians will follow their leader blindly. However, human nature sometimes is unpredictable and this strategy may not always work. Until someone comes up with a gentle solution to the problem of group attacks, some members of the group may have to be injured.

In the event that a Hakko-ryu student is attacked by a group of assailants with weapons, he should again use his common sense and injure some of them, if they cannot be discouraged gently. It is easy to gently disarm one assailant at a time, but gentle techniques **may be** ineffective against a group with weapons. Therefore, it may be advantageous, in the exceptional circumstances of a group attack with weapons, to disarm the leader and threaten to us the weapon against the rest of the group. The fact that you are holding the weapon may discourage a few of the members of the group. If you are forced to use it to wound a member of the group, more members will be discouraged. Therefore, advanced Hakko-ryu students, who understand gentleness well, should be familiar with the use of weapons. To familiarize a person who is not conditioned to gentleness with weapons is dangerous.

COMBAT SITUATIONS

Hakko-ryu Ju Jutsu, with its peaceful philosophy, naturally deplores war. If everyone lived by the Hakko-ryu philosophy of no attack, there would be no war. However, this possibility is not likely in the foreseeable future, therefore there may be war.

The perfect weapon for a country defending against enemy attack, police dealing with rioters and individuals dealing with assailants is gentle technique. A gentle spirit instilled in all men will drive

them to use gentle methods of self defense. There are gentle techniques for police in coping rioters, as there are for soldiers in capturing enemies. One example that many people are familiar with is tear gas. There are many less famous tools of gentleness. Scientists and psychologists are inventing new gentle self-defense methods all of the time. Military scientists devise tactical procedures that will put an enemy army at such a disadvantage that they have no option except to surrender.

The safety of one's country and countrymen should be priority concerns to military leaders. From the humanitarian point of view, the health and safety of the enemy should be of secondary importance. Therefore, military commanders should be as gentle as possible with the enemy. Superiors give the orders and underlings carry them out. The underlings have no option between killing and not killing in war. They must do what their superiors tell them. Therefore, it is the military commanders who should be knowledgeable of gentle tactical maneuvers.

HAKKO-RYU TECHNIQUES ARE NOT DEADLY WEAPONS

In some states, all black belt holders are considered deadly weapons because of the deadly techniques they know. Black belt holders in Hakko-ryu Ju Jutsu know no more deadly techniques than

Philosophy and Intent

the average citizen. There are no deadly techniques in Hakko-ryu. As a matter of fact, students of Hakko-ryu are taught how not to injure assailants. This is what the art is all about. Students are taught only to defend themselves without injuring assailants. A law which considers Hakko-ryu techniques deadly weapons could not be further from the truth. It is quite obvious from observation alone that Hakko-ryu techniques are more harmless than self-defense techniques that the average person untrained in martial arts would use in self-defense situations. This is to say nothing about the mental attitude which is developed by Hakko-ryu students.

Fundamental Principles

THERE ARE FEW FUNDAMENTAL PRINCIPLES that are a major part of many Hakko Den Shin Ryu Ju Jutsu techniques. The five main fundamental principles of the gentle techniques are; stance, balance, ate-mi waza (light striking to body techniques), yielding, and gakun (type of hand movement). Proper stance is necessary to accomplish techniques from the standing position. A knowledge of balance is used mainly in throwing techniques; the sharp pain of ate-mi waza is used primarily to stun assailants. Part of Ju is yielding to strength. Gakun is the unique method of Hakko Den Shin Ryu for capturing and controlling assailants.

STANCE, BALANCE, AND YIELDING

Stance, balance, and yielding are directly related to one another. Many assaults are surprise attacks; therefore, for these situations one may not be in a balanced stance. However, when a person senses the probability of an assault, he can assume a balanced stance by spreading his feet to shoulders' width – one foot behind the other – with his front foot pointing at the assailant and his rear foot pointing away from the assailant.

The balance of an assailant can be broken by gently pushing, pulling, or a push-pull combination. Since Hakko Den Shin Ryu students do not rely on strength, unbalancing procedures are accomplished by yielding to the assailant's strength and using his strength to the user's advantage.

ATE-MI WAZA

At Hakko Den Shin Ryu Honbu

(Headquarters) in Akron, Ohio Mr. La-

Monica teaches a secondary art that defends

against attacks for "within" the body. This

art is Shiatsu igaku (finger pressure medi-

cine). Shiatsu, a process of diagnosing and

treating body ailments, evolved from Chi-

nese acupuncture, one of the oldest medical practices. The method of treatment by Shiatsu is of

great importance in the understanding of Hakko Den Shin Ryu gentle striking techniques.

Shiatsu treatment requires the touching of the various lines in the body that supposedly

lead to the primary organs of the body. The touching of these lines stimulates the correct hormone

activity, which is necessary for the proper functioning of the organs. The treatment is very painful

for someone who is not relaxed. For the relaxed, the treatment is practically painless. As far as

ruffians who attack the outside of our body are concerned, they will be using strength and not be

relaxed. Therefore, if finger pressure is delivered to the "healing lines" of an assailant's body, he

will experience sharp pain, but no injury. Finger pressure applied in self-defense situations is

called ate-mi waza (light striking to body techniques).

The lines can most easily be described as nerves and muscles. It is most important that pressure be applied to the lines where the assailant is concentrating his strength. Ate-mi waza will not be effective if pressure is applied to the relaxed areas of the body. Hakko Den Shin Ryu ate-mi waza is contrary to the traditional ate-mi waza used in other budo schools, which is vicious striking to vital or weak points in the anatomy where the most possible damage can be done. A weak point might be the eye, throat, or groin.

In most cases, it will be possible to touch the appropriate line; however, when assailants move very quickly, it is sometimes necessary to lightly strike the lines. Light strikes, like the touches, are directed to the location of strength.

A different type of ate-mi waza is applied to the face of an assailant. To strike the face without injuring the assailant, a gentle stunning technique must be used. When there is an opportunity to strike an assailant in the face, relax your wrist and fingers completely and snap to the face with the back of your fingers. The harmless pain of this ate-mi waza is enough to discourage an attack, stun the assailant for a few seconds, or cause his eyes to water.

GAKUN

The Hakko Den Shin Ryu grip is believed to be stronger and surer than any other style of grip.

Fundamental Principles

The power of the little finger, which makes a strong grip possible, is accentuated; and the forefinger, which is the least important for a strong grip, is extended. One must use the Hakko Den Shin Ryu grip to accomplish the key movement of the gentle Dori (arts of controlling and capturing), which is called Gakun.

Gakun (type of hand movement), is accomplished by dropping your hand from a level position and squeezing with your little finger. A student of Hakko Den Shin Ryu initially uses gakun to bend the wrist of an assailant. Later, he learns to use the gakun to apply a type of ate-mi waza to the wrist of an assailant.

Wrist bends, applied with gakun, are not wrist twists. Twisting requires more strength than bending. Additionally, the bending of the wrist invokes sharp pain, like the touching of the lines for ate-mi waza; but twisting invokes dull pain, like vicious blows to the body. Wrist twisting and vicious blows my cause serious injury, while wrist bending and gentle ate-mi waza do not cause serious injury.

BASIC TECHNIQUES AND VARIATIONS

Hakko Den Shin Ryu techniques are taught as a progressive system. The novice begins learning the techniques from the kneeling position so that his only worry is his hand movement. Later, he rises to his feet and learns to coordinate hand and leg movements. All of the techniques are extremely simple to learn, providing that the student understands what he is doing and why he is doing it.

ORGANIZATION

The training system is broken down into five dans (degrees). The novice begins studying the first techniques of the first degree, then progresses step-by-step. There are only 21 "basic" techniques in the sho dan (first degree). Every "basic" technique contains important principles that can and should be used in many different self-defense situations. These principles, coupled with fundamentals provide the nucleus for a countless number of techniques. A black belt is awarded after the sho dan "basic" techniques and principles are mastered.

Since Hakko Den Shin Ryu does not waste time with complicated techniques or the instruction of attack for competition and the building of strength, Mr. Okuyama believes that his art is twice as easy as other budo arts. Therefore, black belt training in Hakko Den Shin Ryu should be earned in half the time that it has been traditionally awarded in competition minded budo schools. There usually are ten degrees of training in most budo arts, but in Hakko Den Shin Ryu there are only five degrees. Those who earn the fifth degree replace their black belts with purple

belts- the color of royalty and honor in Japan- and are call Shihan (Master Instructors). Some Shihan, who are selected to be trained more extensively are awarded the grade of Renshi (Fraternal Brothers or Senior Masters); Kaiden (Master of the Deepest Mysteries); San Dai Kichu (Three Great Pillars), the highest title a student can receive, has been awarded to a handful of Mr. Okuyama's followers. (Mr. Michael J. LaMonica was the first non-Oriental to receive the title of San Dai Kichu.) Mr. Okuyama, being the Soke (Originator), went by no other title and wore a purple belt.

LIST OF HAKKO DENSHIN RYU "BASIC" TECHNIQUES

The names, translations and major principles of the first four degrees of Hakko Denshin Ryu "basic" waza (techniques) are presented in the following list. This is the same list of "basic" techniques taught at Hakko Ryu Honbu in Omiya City, Japan.

ShoDan (First degree)

Shodan is the most important of all the degrees. Basic movements are taught, so the same movements can be used with the principles of the upper degrees. To get the new students accustomed to locating the principles of the "basic" techniques, the major principles of "each" basic shodan techniques should be committed to memory.

Shodan Basic Waza

Suware (Kneeling)	English Translation	Principle
1. Hakko Dori	Eighth Light Art	Hakko Dori (Escaping)
2. Atemi	Strike to Face & Body	Atemi Waza
3. Aiki Nage	Spirit Throw	Nage
4. Te Kagami	Hand Mirror	Te Kagami (Hold Itself)
5. Hiza Gatame	Knee Seizure	Atemi
6. Ude Osae Dori	Shoulder Seizure Pin Art (Upper Arm)	Osae Dori (Sho Dan Wrist Bend)
7. Mune Osae Dori	Lapel Seizure Pin Art	Osae Dori
8. Uchi Komi Dori	Strike Inside Art	Osae Dori

Han Tachi (Half Standing)

9. Yoko Kata Te Osae Dori (Yoko Dori*)	Side, One Handed Seizure Pin Art (Side Art)	Ni Ho Nage (Two Way Throw)
10. Kiza Moro Te Osae Dori (Kiza Dori*)	Side, Two Handed Seizure Pin Art (Chair Art)	Ni Ho Nage (Two Way Throw)

Tachi (Standing)

11. Hakko Zeme	Eighth Light Attack	Stance
12. Tachi Ate	Strike	Atemi
13. Hiki Nage	Pull Throw	Nage
14. Te Kagame	Hand Mirror	Te Kagami
15. Ude Osae Dori	Shoulder Seizure Pin Art	Osae Dori
16. Mune Osae Dori	Chest Seizure Pin Art	Osae Dori
17. Ryu Ude Osae Dori	Both Shoulders Seizure Pin Art	Osae Dori
18. Ryu Mune Osae Dori	Both Lapels Seizure Pin Art	Osae Dori
19. Uchi Komi Dori	Strike Inside Art	Osae Dori
20. Ushiro Zeme (Otoshi)	Rear Attack Drop	Otoshi (Drop)
21. Kubi Shime Dori	Neck Choke Art	Introduction to Ni Dan Wrist Bend

Commonly used abbreviated version of the preceding basic waza.

Nidan Basic Waza

Suware (Kneeling)	English Translation	Principle
1. Matsuba Dori	Pine Needle Art (Thumb)	Matsuba Dori
2. Te Kagami	Hand Mirror	Te Kagami
3. Ude Osae Dori	Shoulder Pin Art	Nidan Osae Dori
4. Mune Osae Dori	Lapel Pin Art	Nidan Osae Dori
5. Uchi Komi Dori	Strike Inside Art	Nidan Osae Dori
6. Konoha Gaeshi	Leaf Turnover	Konoha Gaeshi
7. Aya Dori	Cross Pin/ Woven Cloth Art	Aya Dori

Han Tachi (Half Standing)

8. Mae Ryo Te Osae Dori	Front two hand Seizure Pin Art	Ni Ho Nage

Tachi (Standing)

9. Maki Komi	Winding Inside	Maki Komi
10. Te Kagami	Hand Mirror	Te Kagami
11. Shuto Jime	Knife Hand Lock	Shuto Jime
12. Ryo Shuto Jime	Two Hand Seizure Knife Hand Lock	Shuto Jime
13. Ude Osae Dori	Shoulder Pin Art	Nidan Osae Dori
14. Mune Osae Dori	Lapel Seizure Pin Art	Nidan Osae Dori
15. Ryo Ude Osae Dori	Two Hand Shoulder Seizure Pin Art	Nidan Osae Dori
16. Ryo Mune Osae Dori	Two Hand Chest Seizure Pin Art	Nidan Osae Dori
17. Mune Konoha Gaeshi	Lapel Seizure Leaf Turnover	Konoha Gaeshi
18. Kata Te Osae Aya Dori	One Hand Seizure Cross Pin or Woven Cloth Art	Aya Dori
19. Uchi Komi Dori	Strike Inside Art	Nidan Osae Dori
20. Mae Ni Ho Nage	Front Two Way Throw (Opponent goes to his front)	Ni Ho Nage
21. Ushiro Ni Ho Nage	Rear Two Way Throw (Opponent goes to his rear)	Ni Ho Nage

PRINCIPLES
1. Aya Dori   2. Shuto Jime 3. Konoha Gaeshi
4. Nidan Osae Dori 5. Ni Ho Nage   6. Maki Komi

Sandan Basic Waza

Suware (Kneeling)	English Translation	Principle
1. Ude Osae Dori	Shoulder Pin Art	Mochi Mawari
2. Mune Osae Dori	Lapel Pin Art	Mochi Mawari
3. Uchi Komi Dori	Strike Inside Art	Gakun
4. Te Kagami	Hand Mirror	Gakun
5. Aya Dori	Cross Pin/ Woven Cloth Art	Gakun

Han Tachi (Half Standing)

6. Yoko Kata Te Osae Dori	Side Art	Maki Komi
7. Yoko Moro Te Osae Dori	Two Hand Pin Art	Te Kagami
8. Ushiro Gyaku Kubi Jime Dori	Rear Reverse Neck Choke Art	Gakun/ Mochi Mawari

Tachi (Standing)

9. Ryo Mune Osae Dori	Two Hand Lapel Pin Art	Mochi Mawari
10. Emon Dori	Top Of Shoulder Art	Mochi Mawari
11. Te Kagami	Hand Mirror	Te Kagami
12. Uchi Komi Dori	Strike Inside Art	Gakun
13. Tsu Kimi Dori	Thrust To Body Art	Gakun
14. Kata Mune Osae Mochi Mawari	One Handed Chest Pin Lead Around	Mochi Mawari
15. Ryo Te Mochi Mawari	Two Hands Lead Around	Mochi Mawari
16. Ushiro Zeme Dori	Rear Attack Art	Mochi Mawari
17. Ushiro Emon Dori	Rear Shoulder Art	Mochi Mawari
18. Ushiro Obi Hiki Dori	Rear Belt Pull Art	Mochi Mawari
19. Mae Obi Hiki Dori	Front Belt Pull Art	Mochi Mawari
20. Nuki Uchi Dori	Sword Draw Strike Art	Gakun
21. Tsukomi Dori	Thrust Inside Art	Gakun
22. Ushiro Hakko Dori	Rear Eighth Light Art	Mochi Mawari

PRINCILPLES

1. Mochi Mawari   2. Gakun   3. Maki Komi 4. Te Kagami

Yondan BasicWaza

Suware (Kneeling)	English Translation	Principle
1. Mune Osae Dori	Lapel Seizure Pin Art	Shibori
2. Ude Osae Dori	Shoulder Seizure Pin Art	Shibori
3. Emon Osae Dori	Top Of Shoulder Pin Art	Shibori
4. Te Kagami	Hand Mirror	Shibori

Han Tachi (Half Standing)

5. Yoko Dori	Side Art (Attack)	Shibori
6. Yoko Ninin Dori	Side Two Man Art	Shibori

Tachi (Standing)

7. Mune Dori	Lapel Seizure Art	Shibori
8. Ushiro Zeme Dori	Rear Attack Art	Shibori
9. Ushiro Hakko Dori	Rear Eighth Light Art	Shibori
10. Uchi Komi Dori	Strike Inside Art	Shibori
11. Yokomen Uchi Dori	Side of Face Strike Art	Shibori
12. Oikake Dori	Chase After Art	Shibori
13. Heiko Dori	Parallel Art	Shibori
14. Kote Gaeshi Dori	Wrist Turnover Art	Shibori
15. Nuki Uchi Dori/ Shiraha Dori*	Sword Blade Strike Art/ White Blade Art	Shibori
16. Tsu Komi Dori/ Shiraha Dori*	Blade Thrust Art/ White Blade Art	Shibori

Sharp blade edges are "white"- should be done with a live blade.

PRINCIPLES

1. Shibori

Application of Principles

For the sake of uniformity in all of the Hakko Den Shin Ryu Dojos throughout the world, every student must do the basic techniques of each degree in the manner originally set forth by Mr. Okuyama. It is not essential that each Hakko Denshin Ryu instructor apply the techniques to self defense situation in the same fashion. In the Sho dan, for example, every Hakko Denshin Ryu black belt holder must do the same basic techniques of that degree alike. But applications of the principles, fundamentals and variations of the basic techniques to self defense situations are expected to be different, yet similar, from dojo to dojo.

In order for a student to understand the principles, he must practice variations of the required "basic" techniques. The mastery of a minimum of 40 and a maximum of 60 variations should be required of each student, with each degree of basic techniques. The variations should fit the student. This means that most of the variations that are required of a policeman should be the type that he will use in his line of work. A woman should learn to apply Hakko Den Shin Ryu principles to the type of self-defense situations with which women are most often confronted. When a student can use the principles that he knows in many different self-defense situations, it shows that he is grasping an understanding of the principles.

All black belts should be able to use Hakko Den Shin Ryu terminology to name every variation that they do teach, except for police techniques. If the translations of the basic tech-

niques in the preceding list are studied along with the basic techniques themselves, a naming system for variations can easily be developed. The best approach to follow, in naming variations, is fist to name the direction of the attack, second the method of the attack, and third the Hakko Den Shin Ryu technique or principle of defense. It may sometimes be necessary to name the body position of the user of the variation, before naming the variation.

- Basic Waza   A series of techniques performed for form, as a method of learning and teaching.

- Principles   The major ingredients of each Waza.

- Variations   The application of Hakko principles to the Self defense situations.

Application of Principles

Possible Body Position Terms
Suware
Han Tachi
Yokotawaru (Lying)
Tachi

Possible Method of Attack Terms
Akushu
Geri
Kata-te
Kata-ude
Kata-emon
Kata-kubi shime
Kata-ashi
Kata-kami
Kata-obi
Kata-yubi
Kaban
Ko-te
Oikake
Ryo-te
Ryo-ude
Ryo-mune
Ryo-emon
Ryo-kubi shime
Ryo-ashi
Ryo-kami
Ryo-yubi
Moro-te
Moro-ude
Moro-mune
Moro-emon
Moro-ashi
Moro-obi
Tsukomi
Uchi komi
Nuki Uchi
Gun
Chair
Stick
Any weapon

Variation naming combination:
Example: Tachi Mae kata-te osae dori.

Possible Direction of Attack Terms

Mae
Yoko
Ushiro

Possible Hakko Den Shin Ryu Techniques or Principles of Defense

Shodan

Hakko Dori
Atemi Waza
Te Kagami
Osae Dori (Shodan wrist bend)
Ni Ho Nage
Nage
Otoshi

Nidan
Osae Dori (Ni dan wrist bend)
Konoha Gaeshi
Maki Komi
Aya Dori
Ni Ho Nage

Sandan
Osae Dori (Gakun)
Te Kagami
Mochi Mawari

Yondan
Osae Dori (Shibori)

*Police techniques may be taught with English terminology.

HAKKO DENSHIN RYU

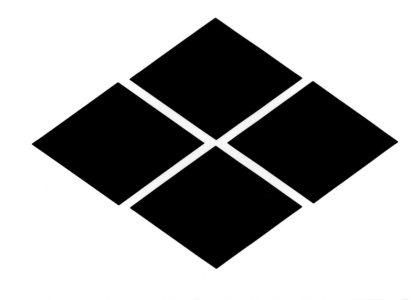

SHODAN WAZA

初
段
技

Hakko Dori

八光捕

1.1.1 Tori and Uke begin in suware. Kneel facing each other, palms placed flat on your own knees, with your knees at least one fist width apart.

1.1.2 Uke reaches across and grabs your wrists, using the Hakko grip.

Hakko Dori

八光捕

1.1.3 Spread the fingers of both your hands, thus increasing the size of your wrists, and rotate your wrists so that your thumbs point up. "Cock" your hands upward at the wrists. Reach for your ears in a circular motion, pushing your elbows toward uke's face. Keep your elbows close to your side as you bring them up behind your ears.

POINTS TO REMEMBER:
- Relax
- Spread your fingers
- "cock" your hands to the inside
- "Reach behind your ears"
- Push through the elbows

Atemi

当て身

1.2.1 Tori and uke begin in suware.

1.2.2 Uke reaches across and grabs your wrists, using the Hakko grip.

Atemi

当て身

1.2.3 Turn your left hand palm upward and use the back of this hand to trap the back of uke's right hand against your left thigh. Spread the fingers of your right hand, "cock the wrist, and reach for your left ear, keeping the palm of your hand toward the floor as much as possible.

1.2.4 Strike the meridian tankei on the right side of uke's neck with a shuto (knife-edge) blow. Alternately, you may strike uke across the face and eyes using metsubushi (a loose-wristed snap with the fingernail side of the fingertips.

POINTS TO REMEMBER:
- Strike tankei on the rear quarter of uke's neck, behind the midline of his neck.

Aiki Nage

合気投

1.3.1 Tori and uke begin in suware.

1.3.2 Uke reaches across and grabs your wrists, using the Hakko grip.

Aiki Nage

合気投

1.3.3 Spread the fingers of your right hand and bend your wrist so that the back of your hand contacts the palm of uke's left hand. Turn your right hand so that your little finger is up and your thumb is down. Simultaneously turn your left hand palm upward and use the back of this hand to trap the back of uke's right hand against the upper inner part of you left thigh. Bend forward to your right and "scoop" your right hand forward along the mat until it is below uke's left hip. Push your right hand into uke's hip and up toward uke's left armpit, throwing uke onto his right side.

1.3.4 Strike uke lightly on the meridian tankei, along uke's right side.

POINTS TO REMEMBER:
- Move both hands simultaneously.
- Lean forward to the side of the forward reaching hand.

Te Kagami

手鏡

1.4.1 Tori and uke begin in suware.

1.4.2 Uke reaches across and grabs your wrists, using the Hakko grip.

Te Kagami

手鏡

1.4.3 On-balance uke by raising both hands onto their fingertips. Spread both hands and move them to the outside, little fingers up. As your opponent pulls his hands back in move your hands back to the center of your body with your palms facing you. Place your left hand in front of your face with the wrist bent so that you are looking into your palm as if it were a hand mirror.

1.4.4 With your right hand, reach under uke's hands and grip uke's right thumb base. Push down and toward uke with the back of your left hand and bend uke's right wrist by bending your right wrist, so that uke's right wrist is bent back toward him. Straighten your right elbow. Ideally, trap uke's right elbow in the pit of his stomach.

Te Kagami

手鏡

1.4.5 Place the knife-edge of your left hand against the back of uke's right hand, just below the knuckles of his first two fingers. Straighten your left elbow. Pull with your right hand as you push with your left hand, thus "locking" uke's right wrist using opposing (push/pull) pressure.

1.4.6 Turn uke's wrist to the outside with your right hand as you rotate your left hand around the back of uke's hand to his little finger knuckle. Throw uke onto his back at your left side. Retain his hand with your right hand as you strike a shuto blow or metsubushi to his face.

POINTS TO REMEMBER:
- Trap uke's elbow in the pit of his stomach.
- Use opposing (push/pull) pressure to "lock" uke's wrist.

Hiza Gatame

膝
固

1.5.1 Tori and uke begin in suware.

1.5.2 Uke reaches across and grabs your wrists, using the Hakko grip.

Hiza Gatame

1.5.3 Turn both hands upward. Use the back of your right hand to trap the back of uke's left hand against your left thigh. Use your left hand to drop the back of uke's right hand onto the joint at the base of uke's left thumb. Press down with your left hand and press up with your right hand. Rotate your right wrist out of uke's grip, toward your abdomen.

1.5.4 Chamber your right wrist at your side and use your fore-knuckle or the flat of your thumb to strike uke on the meridian ikei on his chest. If uke is bent over too far permit this, then strike uke on the meridian tankei on his left side.

POINTS TO REMEMBER:
- Use opposing (up/down) pressure to negate uke's grip on your wrist.
- Roll/rotate hand free.

Ude Osae Dori

腕押捕

1.6.1 Tori and uke begin in suware.

1.6.2 Uke reaches out with his left hand and grabs tori by the right upper sleeve. He then draws back his right fist to punch tori. Simultaneously, bend at the waist to your right side to avoid uke's punch and bring your left hand up straight from your left knee and metsubushi uke across the face. Slide the knife edge of your left hand down uke's left arm and pin uke's left hand to your right arm.

Ude Osae Dori

腕押捕

1.6.3 To off-balance uke, simultaneously sit up straight again and push your right shoulder (not right arm) first toward uke's left shoulder then diagonally toward uke's right shoulder. Raise your extended right arm to a 45 degree angle, little finger up, and begin to "sweep" your arm between you and uke. Simultaneously, gakun uke's left wrist, pivot toward your left knee, and lean forward slightly, thus putting pressure on uke's right wrist and dropping uke's left shoulder toward the mat. (To gakun, pull with your little finger and push with the base of your thumb against uke's wrist while simultaneously dropping your left shoulder and elbow and "pulling with your elbow toward your left hip.) If need be, re-orient your body so that it is perpendicular to uke's arm. Gakun straight down through uke's wrist while leaning your body into the top (index finger portion) of uke's hand. Uke then will be forced to turn his wrist over into the osae dori pin position.

1.6.4 Once uke is in position, maintain pressure on his wrist while arcing his arm down to the mat so that his wrist is above the level of his shoulder, his palm toward his head. Turn toward your left so that you are facing uke's arm with your right leg against his body and both knees near and perpendicular to his arm

Ude Osae Dori

腕押捕

1.6.5 Rotate uke's palm to the mat. Push the back of his hand so that his wrist bends as much as possible toward his head. Slip your thumb down behind uke's hand, pull with your little finger and push with the base of your thumb against uke's hand and attempt to touch the base of uke's fore-finger and palm to the mat near his hand. Release the pressure when uke taps out.

POINTS TO REMEMBER:
- Keep uke's hand in contact with your body until his wrist turns over into the pin.
- Focus the pressure from your gakun, pivot and lean onto uke's wrist joint.
- Maintain pressure on uke's wrist joint.
- The pressure you put on uke's wrist will lead him to choose to turn his hand into the pin position to avoid the pain and possible damage to his wrist. Do not turn his hand over into the pin position using your hand!

Mune Osae Dori

1.7.1 Tori and uke begin in suware.

1.7.2 Uke reaches out with his left hand and grabs tori by the lapels. He then draws back his right fist to punch tori. Simultaneously, bend at the waist to your right side to avoid uke's punch and bring your left hand up straight from your left knee and metsubushi uke across the face. Slide the knife edge of your left hand down uke's left arm and pin uke's left hand to your chest.

Mune Osae Dori

胸押捕

1.7.3 To off-balance uke, push with your chest into uke's hand as you sit back up straight. As you do so turn uke's hand over one quarter-turn so that the back of his hand is parallel to the floor, and gakun his wrist so that his thumb and forefinger are held tightly against your chest.

1.7.4 Simultaneously gakun uke's wrist, pivot toward your left, and lean forward slightly, thus putting pressure on uke's wrist and dropping uke's left shoulder toward the mat. (your gakun will start out parallel to the floor, but will come toward the floor as uke turns his hand over in an attempt to escape the pressure.

Mune Osae Dori

胸押捕

1.7.5 The remainder of the technique is performed exactly as in ude osae dori.

POINTS TO REMEMBER:
- The off-balance push is done with the chest.
- Uke's hand should contact your chest on its thumb and fore-finger side.

Uchi Komi Dori

打込捕

1.8.1 Tori and uke begin in suware.

1.8.2 Uke strikes down toward tori's head using the knife-edge of his left hand. Tori blocks uke's strike in front of tori's forehead using the knife edge of tori's left hand against the underside of uke's wrist. Simultaneously, strike upward with tori's right hand against the underside of uke's left armpit, straightening tori's right arm as as tori does this movement.

Uchi Komi Dori

打込捕

1.8.3 Extend tori's left arm out toward uke's rear to off-balance uke. Continuing this motion, bend your wrist so as to create a "hook" to guide uke's hand down toward your left hip. Simultaneously, push uke's left shoulder in an upside down "U" with your right hand, driving his shoulder toward the mat.

1.8.4 Slide your left hand up the back of uke's left hand so that your fingers are gripping the base of his thumb and your palm is resting against the back of his hand. Turn toward your left so that you are facing uke's arm, with your right leg against his body and both knees against his arm.

Uchi Komi Dori

打込捕

1.8.5 With uke's fingers perpendicular to the mat, push with the meat of your thumb on the back of uke's hand so that his wrist bends as much as possible toward his head. Release the pressure when uke taps out.

POINTS TO REMEMBER:
- Use uke's energy and momentum to drive him to the mat.
- Guide uke's wrist to your hip; do not grab it.

Yoko Kata Te Osae Dori

横片手押甫

1.9.1 Tori and uke begin in the han tachi position. Uke stands at your right side, reaches out with his left hand, grabs tori's right wrist, and pulls. Tori bends his right arm, elbow downward, and drops his weight slightly into his elbow, so that uke cannot pull it straight out. Tori moves his left knee to his right knee, and then moves his right knee to uke's left foot.

1.9.2 Tori bends his right wrist so that his fingers point down; reach across with tori's left hand and grip uke's left hand, palm to palm, with your little finger on his little finger knuckle. Pull down with your left hand and turn your right hand up so that your right palm faces uke and your fingers point up to uke's armpit.

Yoko Kata Te Osae Dori

横片手押捕

1.9.3 Raise your right forearm, allowing it to become nearly vertical and point your right little finger toward uke's left armpit. The pressure on uke's wrist will cause him to rise onto his toes.

1.9.4 Reach for your right ear, leading with your left fore-finger. Transfer your left hand, holding uke's left hand in it, over your head to your left, bending uke's wrist with gakun as you do so.

Yoko Kata Te Osae Dori

横片手押捕

1.9.5 Keeping your left elbow against your side, drop your left hand down to the mat between your legs, bending uke's wrist with gakun as you do so. Uke's wrist should end up against the side of his neck, with his palm turned back toward you. Pin uke by either: one, applying ate-mi pressure with your extended fore-finger knuckle to the meridian tankei on the left side of uke's neck; two, applying ate-mi pressure with your extended forefinger knuckle to the mastoid process in the hollow of the neck behind uke's left ear lobe; or three, trappping uke's head by plac-ing your right hand against his face, while pulling his right wrist out against the gakun.

POINTS TO REMEMBER:
- Lock uke's wrist, elbow and shoulder by pointing your lit-tle finger toward his armpit.
- Drop uke's wrist all the way to the floor as you bring him around your left shoulder.

Kiza Moro Te Osae Dori

椅座 諸手押捕

1.10.1 Tori and uke begin in the han tachi position. Uke stands at your right side, reaches out with both hands, grabs tori's right wrist, and pulls. Tori bends his right arm, elbow downward, and drops his weight into his elbow, so that uke cannot pull it straight out. Tori yields to uke's pull for an instant, and pulls uke to tori by dropping his elbow to his side when uke comes toward tori to catch uke's balance. Tori reaches across between uke's hands with his left hand to grip uke's left hand, palm-to-palm, with your little finger on his little finger knuckle.

1.10.2 The remainder of the technique is performed exactly as in yoko kata te osae dori. The only difference is that uke will have both hands grabbing tori's right wrist.

Kiza Moro Te Osae Dori

1.10.3 The remainder of the technique is performed exactly as in yoko kata te osae dori. Tori should ignore uke's extra hand.

1.10.4 At this point uke's second hand will have to release tori's wrist.

Kiza Moro Te Osae Dori

椅座 諸手押捕

1.10.5 The pin is performed exactly as in yoko kata te osae dori.

POINTS TO REMEMBER:
*   Use uke's balance to bring him to tori when tori yields to his pull.

Hakko Zeme

1.11.1 Uke and tori start in the tachi position.

1.11.2 Tori and Uke Stand facing each other squarely. Uke reaches out and grabs tori's wrists using the Hakko Grip.

Hakko Zeme

八光捕

1.11.3 Tori steps forward with his left leg into a "T" stance, knees bent, hips turned away from uke. Simultaneously, spread both hands, "cock" both wrists upward, and raise your hands to chest level. Push with the heels of your hands against the middle of uke's palms, so that uke's wrists, elbows, and shoulders "lock." Extend your left arm fully, but extend your right arm only three-quarters of the way. Point the fingers of both hands toward uke's eyes.

1.11.4 Step forward with tori's right foot, bringing your hip around, and extend your right arm fully, pushing uke back. Retract your left arm so that it is extended only three-quarters of the way This reverses your "T" stance.

Hakko Zeme

1.11.5 Step forward with tori's left foot, repeating the action of 1.11.4.

Note: In a self-defense situation, if your attacker's arms bend rather than "lock," drive your fingers into uke's face toward his eyes to off-balance uke back. (In practice however; push with the heels of your hands against uke's collarbones.)

POINTS TO REMEMBER:
- Use the power of your pivoting hips rather than the muscles of your arms.
- Flow through the technique without stopping at any point.

Tachi Ate

立
ち
当

1.12.1 Uke and tori start in the tachi position.

1.12.2 Tori and Uke Stand facing each other squarely. Uke reaches out and grabs tori's wrists using the Hakko Grip.

Tachi Ate

1.12.4 Tori steps forward so that your right foot is perpendicular to and just outside uke's left foot. Simultaneously, spread your right hand and "cock" your wrist to the inside. Shift your weight to your right foot and pull your left foot into nekko dachi ("cat stance"). Simultaneously, perform a hakko dori of your right hand to your ear, as in suware ate.

1.12.4 Strike with the knife-edge of your hand to the meridian tan-kei on the right side of uke's neck

Tachi Ate

立ち当

or

1.12.4 Strike with metsubushi to uke's face.

POINTS TO REMEMBER:
- Use the power from your hips to perform the hakko dori.

Hiki Nage

1.13.1 Uke and tori start in the tachi position.

1.13.2 Tori and Uke Stand facing each other squarely. Uke reaches out and grabs tori's wrists using the Hakko Grip.

Hiki Nage

引
投

1.13.3 Tori steps to his left and lowers himself into kiba dachi ("horse stance"). Simultaneously, pull back with your left hand leading with your fingers, and extend your right arm to uke's hip, with your fingers spread, wrist "cocked," and little finger turned upward so that the back of your hand pushes against the palm of uke's hand.

1.13.4 Throw uke by cicling your arms horizontally around you (left hand to your rear, right hand into uke's hip and up toward his left armpit), as you pivot on your feet so that you face to the left.

POINTS TO REMEMBER:
- Move your arms simultaneously with your power step.
- Throw uke using the power of your hips rather than the muscles of your arms.

Te Kagami

1.14.1 Uke and tori start in the tachi position.

1.14.2 Tori and Uke Stand facing each other squarely. Uke reaches out and grabs tori's wrists using the Hakko Grip.

Te Kagami

手鏡

1.14.3 Tori steps slightly forward and just outside uke's right foot with his left foot. Simultaneously, tori spreads his left hand and pulls slightly down with it toward tori's left foot, leading with his fingers.

1.14.4 Tori brings his left hand up in front of his face, palm toward him to form the "hand mirror," and grasp the base of uke's right thumb with tori's right hand as in suware te kagami.

Te Kagami

三
竞

1.14.5 Push down and toward uke with the back of your left hand and bend uke's right wrist, so that uke's right wrist is bent back toward him. Straighten your right elbow.

1.14.6 Place the knife-edge of tori's left hand against the back of uke's right hand, just below the knuckles of his first two fingers. Straighten tori's left elbow . Tori pulls with his right hand as he pushes with his left hand, thus "locking" uke's right wrist using opposing (push/pull) pressure. Tori lifts his left foot, and lets his weight drop down his left hand and into the back of uke's right hand, thus pressuring uke's wrist even more.

Te Kagami

手
鏡

1.14.7 Tori turns uke's wrist to the outside with his right hand as he rotates his left hand around the back of uke's hand to his little finger knuckle. Let tori's weight continue to drop into uke's wrist. Release uke's hand as tori throws uke onto his back at tori's side, and tori catches his weight on his left foot.

POINTS TO REMEMBER:
- Tori drops his weight into his left hand and thus into uke's right wrist.
- Use tori's weight rather than his muscles to throw uke.

Ude Osae Dori

1.15.1 Uke and tori start in the tachi position.

1.15.2 Uke reaches out with his left hand and grabs tori by the right upper sleeve. He then draws back his right fist to punch tori. Simultaneously bend at the waist to tori's right side to avoid uke's punch, step slightly forward and just outside uke's right foot with tori's left foot, and bring tori's left hand up straight from his side to mestsubushi uke across the face. Slide the knife-edge of tori's left hand down uke's left arm and pin uke's left hand to tori's right arm.

Ude Osae Dori

腕押捕

1.15.3 To off– balance uke, simultaneously stand up straight again and push tori's right shoulder (not arm) first toward uke's left shoulder, then diagonally toward uke's right shoulder. Raise tori's extended right arm to a 45 degree angle, little finger up, and begin to "sweep" tori's arm between tori and uke.

1.15.4 Gakun uke's left wrist, pivot toward tori's left on his left foot, and lean forward slightly, thus putting pressure on uke's left wrist and dropping uke's left shoulder toward the mat. Gakun straight down through uke's wrist while leaning tori's body into the top (index finger portion) of uke's hand. Uke will then "snap" his wrist over into the osae dori pin position. Once uke is in the pin position, maintain pressure on his wrist while arching his arm down to the mat so that his wrist is above the level of his shoulder.

Ude Osae Dori

1.15.5 The first part of the pin is exactly like the suware osae dori pin. Then slide tori's right hand down uke's arm to his hand and grab his thumb with the first two fingers of tori's hand, while placing tori's thumb around uke's wrist. Tori moves to the left so that he is in line with uke's arm. Tori places the ball of his left foot against the back of uke's hand just below his first two knuckles. Tori places his right foot in a "T" stance aligned with uke's arm and his left foot.

1.15.6 Release uke's thumb, stand up, and gently roll the ball of tori's foot over the top of uke's hand until he taps out.

POINTS TO REMEMBER:
- Gakun uke's wrist, pivot on tori's foot, and lean into uke's wrist.
- The pressure tori puts on uke's wrist will lead him to choose to turn his hand into the pin position to avoid the pain and possible damage to his wrist. Do not turn uke's hand over into the pin position using tori's hand!

Mune Osae Dori

胸押捕

1.16.1 Uke and tori start in the tachi position.

1.15.2 Uke reaches out with his left hand and grabs tori by the lapels. He then draws back his right fist to punch tori. Simultaneously bend at the waist to tori's right side to avoid uke's punch, step slightly forward and just outside uke's right foot with tori's left foot, and bring tori's left hand up straight from his side to mestsubushi uke across the face.

Mune Osae Dori

1.16.3 Slide the knife-edge of tori's left hand down uke's left arm and pin uke's left hand to tori's chest. Off-balance uke as in suware mune osae dori. Pivot toward tori's left on his left foot and drive uke to the mat as in suware mune osae dori.

1.16.4. Apply the pin to uke's wrist as in suware mune osae

Mune Osae Dori

胸押捕

1.16.5 Apply a standing foot pin as in tachi ude osae dori.

POINTS TO REMEMBER:
- The off-balance push comes up from your foot.

Ryo Ude Osae Dori

両腕甲甫

1.17.1 Uke and tori start in the tachi position.

1.17.2 Uke reaches out with both hands and grabs tori by both upper sleeves. Step slightly forward and just outside uke's right foot with tori's left foot, and bring tori's left hand up straight from his side to mestsubushi uke across the face.

Ryo Ude Osae Dori

両腕押捕

1.17.3 Bend at the waist to your left side and slide the knife-edge of tori's left hand down uke's left arm and pin uke's left hand to tori's right arm. Off-balance uke as in tachi ude osae dori.

1.17.4 Pivot toward your left on your left foot and drive uke to the mat as in tachi usde osae dori.

Ryo Ude Osae Dori

両腕甲甫

1.17.5 Apply the pin to uke's wrist as in tachi ude osae dori.

1.17.6 Apply a standing foot pin as in tachi ude osae dori.

POINTS TO REMEMBER:
- Work agianst one of uke's arms and ignore the other.
- Metsubushi is "between arms."

Ryo Mune Osae Dori

両
胸
押
捕

1.18.1 Uke and tori start in the tachi position.

1.18.2 Uke reaches out with both hands and grabs tori by the lapels. Tori steps slightly forward and just outside uke's right foot with tori's left foot, and bring tori's left hand up straight from his side to mestsubushi uke across the face.

Ryo Mune Osae Dori

両胸押捕

1.18.3 Tori bends at the waist to his left side and slides the knife-edge of tori's left hand down uke's left arm and pin uke's left hand to tori's chest. Off-balance uke as in tachi mune osae dori. As tori gakun's his left wrist , he drops his left forearm over his left wrist and use this pressure to help drive uke to the mat.

1.18.4 Pivot toward tori's left on his left foot and drive uke to the mat as in tachi mune osae dori.

Ryo Mune Osae Dori

両胸押捕

1.18.5 Apply a standing foot pin as in tachi ude osae dori.

POINTS TO REMEMBER:
- The off-balance push comes up from your foot.
- Metsubushi is "over uke's arms."

Uchi Komi Dori

打
込
捕

1.19.1 Uke and tori start in the tachi position.

4.19.2 Uke strikes down toward tori's head using the knife-edge of his left hand. Simultaneously; step forward and just outside ukes right foot with tori's left foot, block uke's strike in front of tori's forehead using the knife-edge of tori's left hand against the underside of his wrist, and strike upward with tori's right hand against the underside of right arm near his armpit, straightening your left arm as you do so.

Uchi Komi Dori

打
込
捕

1.19.3 Extend tori's left arm out toward uke's rear to off-balance him. Continuing this motion, bend tori's wrist to create a "hook" to guide uke's hand down toward uke's left hip. Simultaneously, push uke's left shoulder in an upside down "U" with tori's right hand, driving uke's shoulder toward the mat, and pivot to tori's left on his left foot.

1.19.4 Slide tori's hand up the back of uke's right hand so that tori's fingers are gripping the base of uke's thumb and tori's palm is resting against the back of uke's hand. Extend tori's left arm fully against uke's right shoulder. Bend tori's right knee, driving uke to the mat so that uke's wrist is above the level of his shoulder. Rotate uke's fingers to the mat. Pin as in suware uchi komi dori.

Uchi Komi Dori

打込捕

1.19.5 Tori rotates ukes fingers into the same pin as suware ude osae dori.

1.19.6 Tori applies a standing foot pin as in tachi ude osae dori.

POINTS TO REMEMBER:
- Use tori's weight rather than his muscles to drive uke to the mat.
- Guide uke's wrist to tori's hip; don't grab it.
- Keep arms straight.

Ushiro Zeme Otoshi

後攻落

1.20.1 Uke stands behind tori and grabs him in a bear hug, pinning tori's arms to his sides. Tori steps slightly forward and to the side with his right foot. Tori also bends his legs at the knees, and spreads his arms out from his sides, Tori locks his elbows and spreads his fingers with his little fingers pointing out.

4.20.2 Tori steps straight forward with his hips until tori's hips touch uke. Tori then bends forward, twisting at the waist, reaching for his own left foot with tori's right hand and for the ceiling with his left hand.

Ushiro Zeme Otoshi

後攻落

1.20.3 Tori throws uke to the mat in front and over his right hip.

POINTS TO REMEMBER:
- Tori drops as he spreads his arms at his sides.
- Tori bends forward and circles his arms at the same time.

Kubi Shime Dori

首〆捕

1.21.1 Start in tachi position. Uke reaches across, crosses his arms, slips his fingers and palms inside tori's collar. Uke presses against the carotid arteries at the side of tori's neck. Uke then pulls with each hand "scissoring" tori's neck. Tori drops his chin onto uke's left hand (On tori's left collar) and smile, tightening tori's neck muscles against the choke. (This is described with the left hand as the bottom or lower hand on the choke.)

4.21.2 Tori steps across with his right foot to just in front of uke's right foot, pivoting on his right foot, so that tori stands perpendicular to uke. As tori does this, he extends both arms, hand spread and little fingers up, and pressure uke's left elbow with tori's right shoulder. (If tori is shorter than uke, he raises his shoulder enough to pressure uke's elbow.)

Kubi Shime Dori

首〆捕

1.21.3 Tori throws uke by stepping forward with his right foot as he bows forward and twists toward his left, pushing his shoulder strongly into uke's elbow.

POINTS TO REMEMBER:
- Always work against the bottom hand of the choke.
- Lock uke's elbow with tori's shoulder.
- Tori throws using the power of his hips as he steps forward.

Ko Ko Do Shiatsu

皇光道　指圧治方学

Introduction to Shiatsu

INTRODUCTION TO SHIATSU

THE WORD "SHIATSU", COMPOSED OF the element SHI (finger) and ATSU (pressure), means method of treating illness with digital compression. Shiatsu is a treatment in which the thumbs are used to apply pressure to certain points in order to correct irregularities of the living body, maintain or improve health, and contribute to the cure of certain illnesses.

PRINCIPLE EFFECTS

Koho Shiatsu, the style of shiatsu taught by Mr. Okuyama, produces three principle effects:

1. **Indirect reaction cure --** Taijo (bends)This effect is gained by applying shiatsu to areas different from the injured part. Indirect reaction cure is accomplished through the number techniques, wherein the body is divided into sets of 12 numbers. For instance, if number 8 of one leg was hurt, shiatsu would be applied to all the number eights of the rest of the body. In Japan, Mr. Benko witnessed a discolored, badly bruised toe regain its natural color with the indirect reaction cure applied to the opposite shoulder.

2. **Chemical reaction cure --** This effect is used to combat sudden illness or injury. Shiatsu is administered around the injured part. The chemical reaction cure is quite similar to the simple rubbing of a bruised area.

3. Refreshing effects -- this effect is used to rid a person of exhaustion. Shiatsu is applied along the lines illustrated on the attached chart.

DIAGNOSTIC TECHNIQUES

There are two primary techniques used to examine a patient:

1. Line-pulse techniques -- The pulse is taken with the index fingers. The beats of each of the pulse points are measured by two-breath time. During the two breaths, each of the pulse points must be registered 8 to 9 beats if the patient is in good health. It the number of beats is less or more than 8 to 9, the patient is not well. A list of rules is used to identify the area of difficulty.

2. Observation -- By observing the patient, one can gain many insights into his/her current state of health. For instance, characteristics of a person who may have a kidney ailment may be pale face, dry nose, too frequent urination, low pep and low spirit.

Introduction to Shiatsu

ACUPUNCTURE: DIAGNOSIS AND TREATMENT

The pulse theory is the most widespread diagnostic technique of the acupuncturist. This method is difficult to grasp and seems very mysterious to the Occidental. By placing three fingers on the radial artery of the wrist, one can ascertain the condition of various organs of the body.

Even in ancient China, the pulse method diagnosis was not the only one. The Chinese physician employed a careful observation of the patient's countenance. Many other techniques also were employed.

When the two active forces within the body, yin and yang, are in disequilibrium, the patient is not healthy. Treatment is required to restore equilibrium.

The Chinese observed that internal disequilibrium, or sickness, manifests itself on or through the skin. Thousands of Oriental physicians, over many centuries, have studied man with unending patience before a system of points or lines, on or under the skin, could be devised and related to various organs. This system has come to be known as the "meridian system." Acupuncturists insert needles to points along the meridians and the shiatsuists press points to regain or maintain equilibrium. The following is a coded translation list of the meridian system used in acupuncture and Koho Shiatsu.

SECRETION GLANDS/LINES OF STIMULATIVE SHIATSU/FINGER-PRESSURE POINTS

➢ One must be very careful in the application of Shiatsu to all lines

➢ Dotted lines refer to bending muscles of the body, also called IN-KEY/Yin lines. Each Shiatsu application must be given to a patient upward from the foot.

➢ Straight lines refer to the stretching muscles of the body, also called YO-KEI/ Yang lines. Each Shiatsu application must be given to a patient downward from the top.

➢ One must examine a patient's pulse to find out efficiency Shiatsu lines for the disease/ illness.

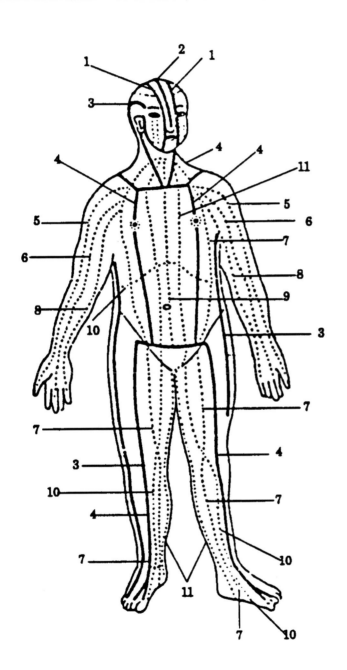

1. BOKO-KEI   bladder line
2. TOKUMYAKU-KEI   Pulse beat line
3. TAN-KEI   Gall bladder line
4. I-KEI   Stomach line
5. HAI-KEI   Lung line
6. SHINPO-KEI   Heart area line
7. HI-KEI   Spleen line
8. SHIN-KEI   Heart line
9. NINMYAKU-KEI   Vein line
10. KAN-KEI   Liver line
11. JIM-KEI   Kidney line

NOTE: One must be extremely careful as to the direction of finger pressure applied to all points except the ones on the torso.

Meridian chart of Koho Shiatsu side of stretching muscles (Back view of the body)

A. BOKO-KEI

Bladder line

B. TOKUMYAKU-KEI

Pulse beat line

C. DIACHO-KEI

Large intestines line

D. TAN-KEI

Gall bladder line

E. SANSHO-KEI

Groin line

F. SHOCHO-KEI

Small intestine line

G. JIN-KEI

Kidney line

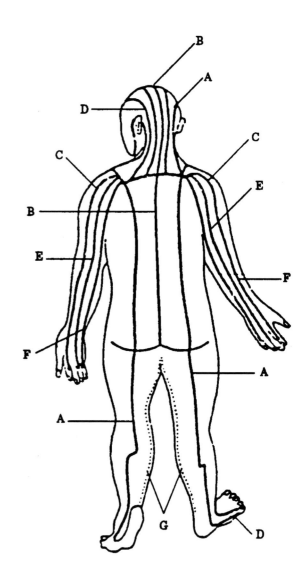

NOTE: One must be extremely careful as to the direction of finger pressure to all points except the one on the torso.

Effectiveness of the secretion line and pulse diagnoses

TOUCH EXAMINATION (man = left /woman = right wrist)

    1.   Shin-Kei   effective for blood circulation

    2.   Kan-Kei   effective for genital organs and nutrition adjustment

3.   Jim-Kei   effective for genital organs and internal secretion

PRESSURE EXAMINATION (man = left /woman = right wrist)

    1.   Shocho-Kei   effective for lifting internal organs

    2.   Tan-Kei   effective for regulating expansion and shrinkage

    3.   Boko-Kei   effective for shrinkage of internal organs

TOUCH EXAMINATION (man = right /woman = left wrist)

    1.   Hai-Kei   effective for blood circulation

    2.   Hi-Kei   effective for nutrition and internal secretion

    3.   Shinpo-Kei   effective for metabolism and regulating circulation

PRESSURE EXAMINATION (man = right /woman = left wrist)

    1.   Daicho-Kei   effective for lifting large intestine and organs

    2.   I-Kei   effective for expansion of internal organs

    3.   Sansho-Kei   effective for lifting muscles and organs

WHERE TO MEASURE A PATIENT'S PULSE FOR KOHO SHIATSU TREATMENT

    1.   Measure width of first joint of thumb (x)

    2.   Using with measurement obtained in Step I, form the first joint of wrist for point (#1)

    3.   Using the same width measure for point (#1), measure points (#2) and (#3)

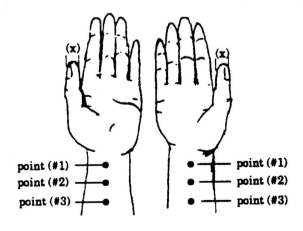

1. Throat/Trachea
2. Lung
3. Heart
4. Liver
5. Gall & outer secretion of pancreas
6. Spleen & internal secretion of pancreas
7. Stomach
8. Kidney
9. Large intestine
10. Small intestine
11. Urinary bladder
12. Genital organs

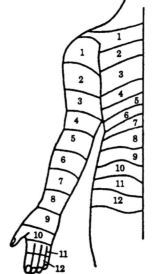

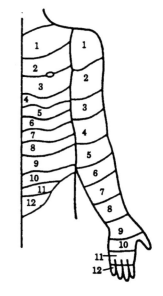

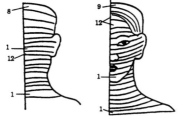

THE SKIN RESPONSIVE LINES
MAKU-HAN-NO-SEN

SHINPO-KEI, SANSHO-KEI, KAN-KEI and TAN-KEI are the lines that cure/ Heal one's illness. Especially, these lines Are effective for serious illness, mental disease and other illnesses that cannot be found from pulse diagnoses.

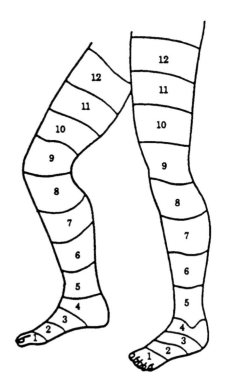

Glossary of Terms

Counting

Ichi	1
Ni	2
San	3
Shi (Yon)	4
Go	5
Rokku	6
Shichi (Nana)	7
Hachi	8
Ku	9
Ju	10
Ju ichi	11
Ni-Ju	20
Ni-Ju-Go	25
Ku-Ju-Hachi	98
Hyaku	100

Colors

Shiroi	White
Midori	Green
Chairo	Brown
Kuroi	Black
Murasaki	Purple

Terminology

Ago	Chin
Akushu	Shaking hands
Arigato	Thank you
Aruite	Walking
Aruku	Walking
Ashi	Legs ankles or feet
Ate	Strike lightly
Ate-mi	Strike body lightly
Aya	Cross pin

Boshi	Hat, cap
Budo	Martial way (Martial arts)
Bujutsu	Martial arts
Bushido	Way of the warrior
Daku	Bear hug
Dan	Grade or degree
Dojo	Practice hall
Dori 1	Hold, seize, capture
Dori 2	Art, technique
Dozo	Please
Emon	Top of shoulder
Empi	Elbow
Eri	Collar
Fushi	Joint, knuckle
Gaeshi	Turn over
Gakun ment	type of hand move-
Gatame	Immobilize, secure
Geri	Kick
Gyaku	Reverse
Ha	Tooth
Hakko	Eighth light
Hana	Nose
Hara	Belly (center of gravity)
Hasami	Scissors
Heiko	Parallel
Henka	Variation
Hidari	The left
Hidari-Gawa	Left side
Hifu	Skin

Glossary of Terms

Hiki	Pull
Hitai	Forehead
Hitasashiyubi	Index finger
Hiza	Lap, knee
Honbu	Headquarters
Igaku	Medicine
(treatment)	
Isu	Chair
Isu Suwari	Chair Sitting
Jime	Lock
Ju	Gentleness, Softness
Jutsu	Art
Kaban	Suitcase, handbag
Kabe	Wall
Kagami	Mirror
Kaiden	Initiate to deepest mysteries
Kakato	Heel
Kamae	Stance
Kami	Hair, paper, god
Kaminoke	Hair
Kamisori	Razor
Kao	Face
Kata 1	Form
Kata 2	One single
Kata 3	Shoulder
Kata-te	Single hand hold on one hand
Koho Shatsu	Particular style of curative massage by finger pressure
Komi	In, inside
Konoha	Leaf (like hand)
Konoha Gaeshi	Leaf turn over
Koshi	Hip, waist

Koshikakete	Sitting
Ko-te	Wrist
Ko-te Gaeshi	Wrist turn over
Koto	Coat
Koyubi	Little finger
Kubi	Neck
Kubi-shime	Neck choke
Kuchi	Mouth
Kurabu	Club
Kusuriyubi	Ring finger
Kutsu	Shoes
Kutsuhimo	Shoelaces
Kutsushita	Socks
Mae	Front
Maki	Wind
Manaka	Middle, center
Matsuba	Pine needle (like thumb)
Me	Eyes
Metsubushi	Thousand warrior (type of atemi)
Migi	The right
Mimi	Ears
Mochi mawari	Lead around
Moro-te	Two-handed hold on one hand
Mune	Chest/Lapel
Nagagutsu	Boot
Nage	Throw
Naifu	Knife
Nakayubi	Middle finger
Naname	Diagonal
Nawa	Rope
Ni	Two, second
Ni-ho	Two way, two direction

Glossary of Terms

Nodo	Throat
Nuki	Drawing of the sword
Nuki uchi	Sword strike (from the draw)
Obi	Belt
Oikake	Chase after
Osae	Seizure
Otoshi	Drop
Oyayubi	Thumb
Pisutoru	Pistol
Rei	Bow
Renshi	Senior Brother
Ryo	Both, two
Ryo-te	Both hands
Ryu	School, style, system
San	Three, third
Sensei	Teacher
Shiatsu	Finger Pressure
Shiatsu Igaku	Finger Pressure medicine
Shibori	Squeeze, pressure
Shihan	Master rank
Shime	Strangle
Shinden	Shrine
Shizo	Heart
Sho	First, basic
Shuto	Knife hand
Sode	Sleeve
Suware	Sitting
Tachi	Standing
Tataku	Roundhouse punch

Te 1	Hand
Tebukuro	Glove
Tobi	Flying
Tsukiage	Upward thrust (upper cut)
Tsukimi	Thrust to body (with hand)
Tsukomi	Thrust to body (as with knife)
Uchi	Strike
Uchi-komi	Strike inside
Ude	Arm, shoulder
Ukemi	Body protecting (falling)
Ushiro	Rear
Uwagi	Jacket
Wa	Peace, Peaceful
Waishatsu	Shirt
Waza	Technique
Yoko	Side
Yokomen	Side of face
Yokotawaru	Laying
Yon	Four, Fourth
Yubi	Fingers
Yudansha	Black belt holder
Zeme	Attack
Zubon	Trousers

Glossary of Terms

Classical Arts of Japan

Ba-Jutsu	The Art of Horsemanship
Batto-Jutsu	The Art of Drawing the Sword
Bo-Jutsu	The Art of the Wooden Staff
Fukimibari-Jutsu	The Art of Blowing Needles
Ho-Jutsu	The Art of Ancient Ginnery
Ju-Jutsu	The Art of Gentleness (unarmed defense)
Jutte-Jutsu	The Art of Sword Defense (with a metal blocking Prong)
Ken-Jutsu	The Art of Aggressive Swordsmanship
Kusarigama-Jutsu	The Art of Chain and Sickle
Kyu-Jutsu	The Art of Archery
Mojiri-Jutsu	The Art of Entanglement (Using a sodegarami-spiked pole)
Naginata	The Art of the Long Halberd
Shinobi-Jutsu	The Art of Stealth and Espionage
Shuriken-Jutsu	The Art of Throwing Spike or Wheel shaped Darts
So-Jutsu	The Art of the Long Spear
SuieiJutsu	The Art of Swimming Clad in Armor
Tanto-Jutsu	The Art of the Dagger
Torite-Jutsu	The Art of Rope Binding and capture (Torinawa-Jutsu or Hojo-Jutsu)

Ju Jutsu once had many other names, such as:

Hakuda	Hakushu	Hakute	Kempo	Kogusoku
Koshi-No-Mawari	Kumiuchi	Shirauchi	Shubaku	Shuhaku
Tai-Jutsu	Teshibari	Torite	Wa-Jutsu	Yawara

Self Defense

THE BEST DEFENSE IS PREVENTION

Prevention is the key to your personal safety. Prevention means being aware of two things:

1. What can happen to you.

2. What you can do to avoid it.

Greater safety lies not in getting out of trouble, but avoiding trouble in the first place. Self-protection means taking all necessary precautions order to reduce minimize or possibly eliminate your chances of becoming a victim of crime.

Never provoke an attack. If it is apparent that it is only your money at stake, give it up, try to remember what he attacker looked like, give as accurate a description as you can to the police. It is impossible to advise you specifically as to what to do if attacked, because only a person under attack is qualified to make this decision. The best way to avoid panic is, of course, to be prepared.

Panic paralyzes you. If you are prepared to meet the emergency of a possible attack, you are more likely to run (when that is the safest procedure) than if you are totally unprepared. Panic prevents us from seeing the possible solution to an emergency situation. Prevention procedures minimize the danger of physical attack. Take precaution- develop safety habits.

Self Defense

Don't forget- the best defense is PREVENTION.

The Dojo

Judo, karate and Ju Jutsu are taught in a school called a "dojo". More than merely a gymnasium or a club, a dojo is a cherished place of learning and brotherhood for the devotees. The word "dojo" implies an even broader meaning. It is symbolic of the methodological, ideological, philosophical and spiritual aspects of martial arts. Thus, the study of judo, karate or jujutsu involves far more than the learning of certain physical techniques. It absorbs the student wholly- his character is as much affected by the training of his body.

The dojo is based on the idea of virtue. Indeed followers of the martial arts today are in effect the descendants of the Samurai of old. It is the aim of the martial arts' masters to work toward the advancement of this spirit of the ancient Zen warrior, a spirit which is much more than mere knowledge of fighting techniques. It is the attainment of a virtuous way of life- the main strive, for only then can a student become a true practitioner of the art.

A traditional dojo is, in a sense, a patriarchy. The sensei is the master of the dojo. "Sensei" is the Japanese word for "honorable teacher". The sensei regards the students as his many sons and daughters, seeing them as they can never see themselves. He affects the development of their bod-

Self Defense

ies and their characters- this is the responsibility of his art. The dojo really is the home of the sensei- students come to his home to learn his way of life. **That way of life is martial arts.** All traditional dojos are created by the sensei and maintain the standards of simplicity and beauty found in original dojos, which always had a shrine built in the highest possible position, symbolizing the dojo's dedication to the virtues and values of it's style. All dojos should have time allotted for the practice of meditation, which aids in developing the spiritual teachings and mental training underlying all the martial arts.

MARTIAL ARTS

Karate: Means "empty hand"

Consists of kicks, punches and striking techniques.

Judo: Means "gentle way"

Consists of throws, reaps, arm bars and chokes

Ju Jutsu: Means "art of gentleness"

Has all the kicks and punches of Karate, the throws and reaps of Judo plus all the wrist-locking and controlling techniques which are unique to Ju Jutsu alone.

Self Defense

Basic Principles

I. A thorough knowledge of the three principles upon which defensive tactics is based is necessary in order to learn and effectively use it.

    A. Balance

        1. It is through a balance position that a maximum of speed, power and accuracy in physical movement can be obtained.

        2. In defensive tactics, the object is to maintain your balance while trying to keep your opponent off balance.

        3. Reasonably good balance is established with the right (or left) foot slightly forward feet spread and knees slightly bent.

        4. Constantly shift the feet in relationship to the direction of the attack.

    B. Stance

        1. Leverage

            a. Has to do with extensive use of the trunk muscles, particularly the abdominal muscles and good body mechanics.

            b. Good body mechanics consists of the use of the proper muscles in the proper way at the proper time. **Proper use of hip rotation and transfer of body weight is needed to manufacture power.**

2. Concentrate your power

    a. All of your power should be concentrated at your opponent's weakest point.

    b. Maximum strength should be used against minimum strength.

C. Yielding- Utilization of opponent's power

1. Use the strength and momentum of your opponent to your advantage.

2. You should assume that your opponent is stronger than you.

    a. You do not oppose him directly, but rather you use your strength to direct his movements.

    b. If he pushes, you pull.

3. Your opponent's momentum, properly directed by you, is the chief factor in bringing about his downfall.

Fundamentals

II. The position which you can best defend yourself, as well as knowledge of how and where to strike counter blows., are the fundamentals of defensive tactics.

A.   **On Guard Position**

Self Defense

1. **Unassuming Posture** (Alert Stance, Interview or Interrogation Stance for Police)

    a. Is used when talking to a person or subject where a possibility of attack exists

    b. Stand about an arms length away, facing him with your body at about a 45-degree angle, strong side turned away.

    c. Your feet are directly under your shoulders or just slightly farther apart, knees bent slightly.

    d. Hands near the center of your body or one or both hands should loosely grasp (thumbs out) the lapels of your coat or your arms should be loosely folded at the chest.

    e. This allows you to go into action quickly and defend yourself against a sudden attack.

2. **Combat Stance**

    a. When you are being attacked, the combat stance should be assumed.

    b. The feet are comfortably spread with the right foot (if you are right handed) about 12" or more to the rear of the left.

c. The knees are slightly bent, with the weight of the body on the balls of the feet.

d. Your hands should be held about face high and elbows should be carried reasonably close to the body.

e. This is a good position of balance from which you can defend and counter attack to the best of your ability.

B. **Personal Weapons**

1. Personal weapons are the parts of the body that can be used for self-defense or counter attack purposes.

    a. "Edge of Hand" or "Edge of Fist". These blows are most effective when delivered with a chopping motion across the body with the palm down or downward with the palm facing in.

    b. "Spear Hand" or "Finger Jab" blows are delivered with the fingers held rigid.

    c. The "Heel of the Hand" blow is delivered upward, when you are close to your opponent.

    d. The foot is used for kicking forward with the ball of the foot, to the side the edge of the foot, ball and heel. Short snapping kicks, using the foot and delivered to your opponents shin or knee are extremely effective in fighting.

e.The elbow should be fully flexed when used as a weapon and the most effective blows are delivered outward across the body or toward the rear.

f. A forearm blow is usually delivered by raising the arm of the shoulder high, flexing the elbow fully and when swinging the arm sharply forward the inside using hip rotation and transferring body weight.

Forearm Smash

S.1.1 The attack begins with the assailants hands are inside your shoulder area. (choke hold) Step back into a defensive stance where you are on balance and ready to defend yourself. Then raise your strong side arm up (humorous bone parallel to the ground).

S.1.2 Pivot on the balls of both feet, all of your body weight using hip rotation, through their elbow and break it, using your forearm to make the contact between your arm and the attacker's elbow.

Forearm Smash

S.1.3 After this, follow through and use your elbow to strike hisunprotected area: face or rib cage and groin.

Anchor and Break

S.2.1 The attack begins with the assailants hands are inside your shoulder area. (choke hold) Just as in "Forearm Smash".

S.2.2 Reach between your attacker's arms and anchor his opposite hand with your hand so it will not come off when you do the technique.

Anchor and Break

S.2.3 Front View: This time use the heel of the free hand to break the elbow as you pivot on the balls of your feet.

S.2.4 Rear View: This time use the heel of the free hand to break the elbow as you pivot on the balls of your feet.

Spear Hand to the Throat

S.3.1 The attack begins with the assailants hands are inside your shoulder area. (choke hold) Just as in "Forearm Smash". Step back into a defensive stance.

S.3.2 Shape your hand like a spear by bringing your fingers together.

Spear Hand to the Throat

S.2.3 Jab the throat area as you pivot your hips and rotate on the balls of your feet transferring your weight into your attacker.

S.3.4 Follow up with a front or side snapping kick.

Intercept the Hands

S.4.1 As the attacker goes to attack you (before the attacker gets a hold of you) step back and intercept his hands with yours and shoot them straight up.

S.4.2 Follow up with a front snapping kick as you pull his hands down to your bottom rib in a jerking motion

Elbow to the Ribs 1

S.5.1 As the attacker goes to grab you in a bear hug, step towards him with a circular motion and strike his bottom ribs with your elbows.

S.5.2 Step back and rake the eyes or scratch his face. This will get his hands to go up.

Elbow to the Ribs 1

S.5.3 Follow up with a front snapping kick.

Elbow to the Ribs II

S.6.1 This time the attacker is too close for you to step forward, therefore you step back as you are striking his ribs.

S.6.2 Step back and rake the eyes or scratch his face. This will get his hands to go up.

Elbow to the Ribs 11

S.6.3 Follow up with a front snapping kick.

Forearm, Knee

S.7.1 As the attacker punches, step up to his outside (toward punching hand) with the same side foot that you will use to deflect the punch (circular inside to outside block). Example: When the attacker punches with his right hand, you block with your left hand while stepping with the left foot.

S.7.2 Strike across the chest with your forearm as hard as you can. (On the street, strike the throat area with the forearm.)

Forearm, Knee

S.7.3 Grab his shoulder with both hands, and knee him in the groin as you pull him down toward the knee.

Foot Sweep

S.8.1 As the attacker punches, step up to his outside (toward punching hand) with the same side foot that you will use to deflect the punch (circular inside to outside block). Example: When the attacker punches with his right hand, you block with your left hand while stepping with the left foot.

S.8.2 Strike across the chest with your forearm as hard as you can. (On the street, strike the throat area with the forearm.)

Foot Sweep

S.8.3 This time take the hand that you used to strike the chest and push his head back while pulling his punching arm to your hip with your left hand. This will make him off balance.

S.8.4 Step through with your right foot to his right side so that you are hip-to-hip. Swing your right leg through, and like a pendulum, sweep his right leg.

Rear Hip Throw from a Bear Hug

S.9.1 The attacker attacks from behind in a bear hug. Lower your center of gravity, and keep your knees slightly bent (Horse Stance). Turn little finger of each hand to the outside. Keep good posture (back straight). Bring your hands and arms up over the attacker's arms and/or hands.

S.9.2 Punch in with your left elbow while punching straight out with your right arm.

Rear Hip Throw from a Bear Hug

S.9.3 Punch in with your right elbow striking him in the solar plexus or groin area as you pivot clockwise on the balls of your feet. Grab his right elbow with your left hand and put your right arm around his waist from the left side of his body.

S.9.4 Make sure your hip is slightly outside and below his hip. Snug him in tightly so there are no gaps around the hip area. Straighten your knees and the attacker should come off the ground.

Rear Hip Throw from a Bear Hug

S.9.5 All that is left is the throw. Do this by rotating your right arm over the top as if to touch your left toe and pulling his right arm across your body with your left arm.

Rear Hip Throw from a Punch Coming from the Front

S.10.1 As the attacker punches, step up to his outside (toward punching hand) with the same side foot that you will use to deflect the punch (circular inside to outside block). Example: When the attacker punches with his right hand, you block with your left hand while stepping with the left foot.

S.10.2 As you strike his groin, step up with your right foot nest to his right foot and make an "L" shape.

Rear Hip Throw from a Punch Coming from the Front

S.10.3 Then you are going to turn counter-clock-wise about 180 degrees so you are facing the same way the attacker is as you place the right arm around his waist and grab his right elbow with your left hand.

S.10.4 This is the same throw as #9.

Front Choke Sit Down Throw/Stomach Throw

S.11.1 Both the attacker and you start out in a left forward stance. The attacker grabs you in a choke hold. You reach inside of the attacker's arms and grab something around the lapel area to hold onto.

S.11.2 You step back with your left foot. The attacker takes a step with his right foot. You are going to sit straight down while the attacker takes a giant step with his left foot up toward your shoulder area. You place either foot on the attacker's right thigh or shin area. (On the street, place or kick with the foot into the groin or stomach area).

Front Choke Sit Down Throw/ Stomach Throw

S.11.3 As the attacker starts to go over, the attacker lets go of the defender and does a shoulder roll to prevent injury. When the attacker starts to go over, you pull with your hands and kick him over by using the foot on his thigh to give him the momentum the attacker needs to complete the roll. (This is for class purposes; other endings will be discussed.)

Acknowledgements

The Hakko Denshin Ryu Ju Jutsu manual was written by Michael J. LaMonica, Kaiden Shihan San Dai Kichu.

Special thanks to the following:

Translations
    Provided by Brian Workman
    Chris Kobak

Photography
    Chris Kobak
    Christine LaMonica

Ukes
    Chris Kobak
    Craig Hanus

Layout, Design, Editing
    Cristine Kobak
    Ken Hoggart
    Chris Kobak

Bibliography
    ** Out Of The Mist, By Brian Workman, <u>Black Belt Magazine</u>.

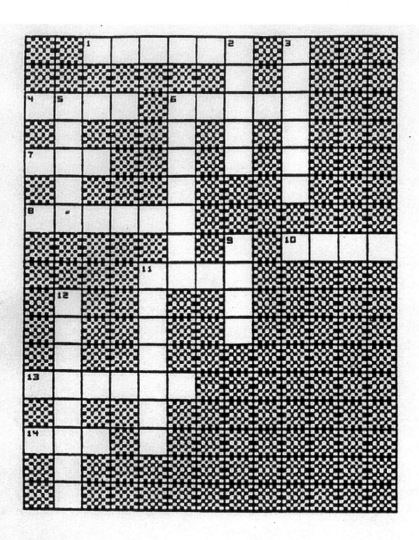

CROSS CLUES

1. THE "JU" IN JUDO MEANS _____.
4. "KARATE" MEANS EMPTY _____.
6. MOST OF THE MARTIAL ARTS
   DISCUSSED HERE COME FROM _____.
7. "DO" IN JUDO MEANS _____.
8. YOU GET YOUR POWER FROM BODY
   _____.
10. "JUTSU" IN JUJUTSU MEANS _____.
11. A SPORT THAT INVOLVES THROWS,
    ARMLOCKS AND PINS _____.
13. A SPORT THAT INVOLVES PUNCHING
    AND KICKING TECHNIQUES IS
    _____.
14. YOU GET YOUR POWER FROM _____
    ROTATION

DOWN CLUES

2. "KARA" IN KARATE MEANS _____.
3. "JU" IN JUJUTSU MEANS _____.
5. IF YOU GET NOTHING ELSE FROM THIS
   COURSE BE _____ OF WHAT IS
   GOING ON AROUND YOU.
6. ORIGINALLY DEVELOPED FOR USE ON
   THE BATTLEFIELD BY SAMURAI
   WARRIORS.
9. YOU GET YOUR POWER FROM _____
   WEIGHT.
11. A MARTIAL ART THAT EMBODIES
    THROWS OF JUDO, STRIKES OF
    KARATE AND WRIST LOCKING TECHS.
12. YOU GET YOUR POWER FROM HIP
    _____.

Instructor Comments and Student Notes

Instructor Comments and Student Notes

Instructor Comments and Student Notes

Instructor Comments and Student Notes